STEAM RAILWAYS

Britain's preservation railways and museums

Navigator Guides Ltd
The Old Post Office, Swanton Novers
Melton Constable, Norfolk NR24 2AJ
postmaster@navigatorguides.com

Copyright © Navigator Guides Ltd 2001

Designed by Ann Burnham
DTP Heath Lodge Publishing Services

First published in hardback 1999
Written by: Joseph Fullman & G.P. Foreman
Additional contributions and research: Joanne Taborn
Completely updated by Yvette Douglas 2001

ISBN 1 903872 00 6

A catalogue record for this book is available from the British Library

Colour reproduction by
C3 Imaging, Newcastle upon Tyne
Printed in Italy by
Printer Trento srl

Photo Credits
The publishers would like to thank all those railway societies and
organisations who supplied photographs for this book with
particular thanks to Graham Kenworthy.
Photographs listed below have detailed copyright:© Robert Williams,
Snowdon Mountain Railway; ©Tony and Linda Beard, Ground Glen; ©
Peter van Campenhout, Lakeside and Haverthwaite; © Avon Valley Railway;
© Geoff Silver, Barrowhill Roundhouse; © Tony Sullivan, Bluebell Railway;
John White, Dean Forest Railway; Gordon Thomson, Scottish Industrial
Centre; Bideford Railway Museum © Rob Dark; ©Darlington Railway
Centre; Dean Forest Railway © John White; North Norfolk Railway © Steve
Allen; Glasgow Museum of Transport © Glasgow Museums; Strathspey
Railway © K. Pirt; Bala Lake, Snowdon Mountain Railway, Teifi Valley
Railway and Welshpool & Llanfair Light Railway © Peter Johnson; Welsh
High Railway © DW Allan

Acknowledgements
The publishers would like to thank Graham Kenworthy and Yvette
Douglas for her invaluable help in the production of this book

CONTENTS

CONTENTS

ISLE OF MAN

SCOTLAND

WALES

4

There is something almost magical about a steam railway. Whether the effect is caused by the smell of hot oil, the sound of excess steam lifting the safety valve or the sight of Thomas the Tank Engine coming to life depends largely on the individual's age or choice of reading material. There are, of course, many other aspects of the operation which may also evoke memories for the older visitor or arouse the curiosity of the young who were born too late to remember the "glory days": the guard's whistle and green flag; the driver's "greasetop" hat and blue overalls; the signalman's spotless signalbox with its levers for setting the points or controlling the signals; the toot or chime of the engine's whistle as the rods and wheels begin to move. These are all things that were once taken for granted, but which are now largely confined to the locations covered by this guide.

Over the last forty years or so, sites of "preserved" railways have become increasingly popular as destinations for a day trip, either from home or as part of a holiday. In the early days of the preservation movement most visitors were "enthusiasts", who had witnessed the rapid decline of the steam locomotive on Britain's railways combined with the closure of a large proportion of the system. More recently, however, although many afficionados are still drawn by the technology, family groups have taken over as the largest visitor category.

Railway Preservation

"Railway Preservation" means many things to many people and any attempt to define precisely when it began can be the starting point for much discussion, not least among the large, but inevitably ageing, band of enthusiasts who can actually remember the early days.

Many will claim that the formation of the Talyllyn Railway Preservation Society in 1950 was the source of the phenomenon. Others will dismiss this assertion by saying that preservation didn't start in earnest until the first successful proposal to re-open a standard gauge line was made in 1959. However, despite the seeming plausibility of both arguments, you will find in the pages of this book a number of examples of private lines that were providing a tourist service several years before either example quoted above; where these earlier lines still survive, they are now accepted under the umbrella title of "preserved railways".

Standard gauge lines

Narrow gauge lines

Miniature lines

Other facilities

It is very difficult to generalise on the origins of the sites now used for preserved steam railways, but the vast proportion of preservation centres using standard gauge (4'-8_") are located on closed British Rail lines or at former industrial sites which had been connected to the national system. The majority of locomotives in use at such locations fall into similar categories. They were either purchased direct from British Rail or industrial operators as they were withdrawn from service, or they were rescued from scrap merchants, sometimes many years after withdrawal. Whatever their source, many of them required large sums of money to be spent before returning to operational use and they continue to consume more money than they do coal!

Disused industrial sites, such as quarries and coal mines, have also been used to establish narrow gauge lines (anything less than 4'-8_", but, in practice, not greater than 3'-0"). There are many narrow gauge branches, each several miles in length, which have an essentially industrial history but which also provided a means of transport for the local population.

Miniature lines can be defined broadly as those which are laid to a narrow gauge, usually 15" or less, but where the locomotives are scaled down versions of main line originals. Not surprisingly, these lines do not have "miniature" carriages because they would not be able to carry full size people! The sites used for these lines vary tremendously; some are laid along closed British Rail routes, some are seaside attractions or in theme parks, some are in the grounds of stately homes and some are provided as an additional feature of large garden centres.

Small museums have been established at a number of locations. These can be of great assistance to those interested in such matters, explaining the history of steam railways in general or of the line in particular, putting it into the context of its original purpose.

Virtually all preserved railways, of whatever category, offer a range of attractions beyond simply the trains themselves, encouraging a broad appeal. In addition to normal opening days, many hold special events on or around specific dates, such as St Valentine's Day, Mothers' Day, Easter, Fathers' Day, Halloween, Bonfire Night, Christmas and New Year. There are also

attractions aimed at the younger end of the market; these may include taking a ride with such celebrities as Thomas the Tank Engine, Postman Pat or the Mad Hatter. Likewise, for the adults (but with the hope that the children will also come along) there are events concentrating on Rail Mail, Model Railways and Railways at War. Those of a gastronomic disposition will find programmes centred on Real Ale, Cream Teas, Mince Pies and Pullman Dining.

Some form of café or restaurant facility is usually provided; indeed some of the larger concerns have found that there is sufficient demand to justify such provision at several stations along the line. Several have also established good quality licensed premises serving real ale as well as wines and soft drinks. Gift shops also feature prominently, selling a wide range of giftware.

Websites are an ever expanding source of information on a hugely diverse range of topics related to preserved railways, not only providing details of these special events, but also listing regular timetables, together with information on access by public transport. For each entry a website address is given where one existed at the time of going to press. The UK Heritage Railways website at www.ukhrail.uel.ac.uk is a valuable source of information.

The sites included here are a vital and flourishing part of the tourist industry and the final routes to many of them are well indicated by the familiar brown road signs reserved for such attractions. Because so much reliance is placed on visitors arriving by road, ample car parking will usually be available. However, special events can place a great strain on such facilities, so "patience" may be the watchword on such occasions. Don't forget that the staff want you to return and will be doing their best to ensure that your visit is enjoyable; most of them will probably be carrying out their duties on a voluntary basis, hoping to enjoy the day as much as you do.

So, whatever your choice, enjoy the magic!

GRAHAM KENWORTHY

8

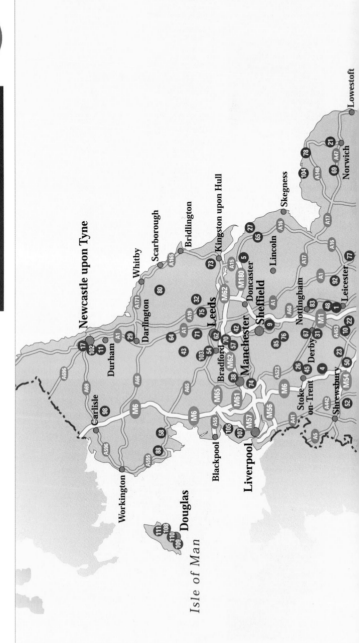

Note:
The railways are numbered in
alphabetical order in accordance
with the contents pages 3-4.

ABBEY PUMPING STATION

HOW TO FIND US:
By car: 1 mile north of
Leicester city centre
Car parking: Free
By rail/bus: Leicester
Station for bus services
Nos 54 and 61, or
Loughborough Station
for Great Central Railway
ADDRESS: The Abbey
Pumping Station,
Corporation Road,
Leicester LE4 5PX
TEL: 0116 299 5111
FAX: 0116 299 5125
LINE LENGTH: 300 yds
OPENING TIMES: Apr–Oct,
10–5 Mon–Sat, 2–5 Sun;
Nov–Mar, 10–4.30 Mon–
Sat, 1.30–4.30 Sun;
Phone for information
on steam event days
FACILITIES: Café only on
special event days
DISABLED: Call ahead

P ART OF THE Museum of Science and Technology for Leicester, the Abbey Pumping
Station has the longest passenger-carrying narrow gauge (2') railway in Leicestershire, originally built for th e clearance of screenings when
it was a sewage pumping station. The railway
line is operated on the many themed steam
days that take place throughout the year. The
Museum has a collection of historic steam
engines, as well as boasting the largest working
beam engines in the country. There is also a
fascinating permanent exhibition "Flushed
with Pride" (a history of public health). Visitors
can also take a 15-minute walk along the river
to nearby Belgrave Hall and Gardens.

AIRFIELD LINE

HOW TO FIND US:
By car: Within Coventry
Airport boundary,
entrance adjacent to
Emergency Exit Gate 2
Car parking: On site,
access off Rowley Road
By rail/bus: Train to
Coventry, then West
Midlands Bus Route
20/21 from city centre
to Toll Bar end
ADDRESS: Rowley Road,
Baginton, Coventry
TEL: 0121 708 2815
evenings/ansaphone
FAX: 0121 707 7330
LINE LENGTH: 660 yds
(under construction)
OPENING TIMES: Easter–
Oct: 11–5 Sun & public
holidays. See press for
special events
DISABLED: Call ahead.
No toilets

T HE ONLY STANDARD gauge line in War-
wickshire, this recently constructed site
was originally known as the Coventry Steam
Railway Centre. Development continues
with the reconstructed 118-year old LNWR
North Kilworth station building and ongoing work on the 6-acre site to create a
tradional railway setting, with the former
MR Little Bowden signalbox and a number
of locomotives as additional attractions.
Volunteers run operating days and special
events. There is also a collection of vintage
road rollers, and the largest collection of
electric traction rolling stock in preservation
in the United Kingdom.

AMBERLEY MUSEUM

HOW TO FIND US:
By car: Amberley
Museum is located on
the B2139

Car parking: Free at
Amberley

By rail: Amberley

ADDRESS: Amberley, nr.
Arundel, West Sussex
BN18 9LT

TEL: 01798 831370

WEBSITE: www.
amberleymuseum.co.uk

LINE LENGTH: 500 yds

OPENING TIMES:
Mar–Nov: 10–6
Wed–Sun; daily during
school holidays

FACILITIES: Café, picnic
tables, gift shop

DISABLED: Wheelchair
access

THIS 36-ACRE open-air museum on the site of the former Amberley Chalk Pits holds one of the most extensive collections of narrow gauge rolling stock in the country – 30 locomotives and over 40 varieties of wagon and coach. There are also two sections of track. The first is an industrial demonstration line, while the second carries passengers nearly half a mile in all–too–authentic (unsprung!) quarrymen's coaches. Elsewhere you can see demonstrations of traditional local crafts such as pottery and cobbling in recreated workshops. Betch-worth Hall houses several locomotives.

AMERTON

HOW TO FIND US:
By car: Amerton is on
the A518

Car parking:
Available on site

By rail/bus: Train to
Stafford, then
Stevenson's of Uttoxeter
Ltd bus to Weston, then
mile walk to Amerton

ADDRESS:
Amerton Railway,
Stowe-by-Chartley,
Staffs ST18 0LA

TEL: 01889 270294

INFOLINE: 01785 850965

LINE LENGTH: 1 mile

OPENING TIMES:
Steamers operate
Jun–Oct: Sun & public
holidays; diesels mid-
Apr–Aug: Sat

FACILITIES: Licensed tea
room and bakery

DISABLED: Call ahead

IN 1987 A GROUP of volunteers came together to rescue and restore "Isabel", a hundred-year-old steam locomotive. They also decided to build her a new home—the 2ft gauge Amerton Railway. Work has continued ever since and in 2001 a new extension will take the line to around a mile in length. Several other engines have joined "Isabel" at Amerton, including an 0-4-2T "Pearl 2", Baguley's "Dreadnought" and "Golspie", and a number of Rustans and MotorRails.

APPLEBY-FRODINGTON

HOW TO FIND US:
Phone for directions
ADDRESS: Appleby-
Frodington Railway
Preservation Society,
P.O. Box 44, Brigg,
North Lincolnshire
DN20 8DW
TEL: 01652 656661
(for enquiries)
01652 657053 (bookings)
E-MAIL:
bookings@afrps.co.uk
LINE LENGTH: 7–15 miles
OPENING TIMES:
Not open except by
prior booking. All tours
run free of charge, but
must be pre-booked as
places are limited
FACILITIES: Buffet, gift
shop and toilets
DISABLED: Disabled
access to train (phone
in advance); toilets

THIS IS A true enthusiast's railway, with rail tours run by members of the society for pre-booked visits. The society is based in the CORUS steelworks at Scunthorpe, which produces about 4 million tonnes of steel a year. There are approximately 90 miles of internal railways on the site. The Society run three rail tours, one of 7 miles and one of 15 miles, both of which include a visit to the loco shed, and a brake van tour which visits parts of the railway system not normally accessible with the passenger coaches.

AUDLEY END

HOW TO FIND US:
By car: Audley End
House, just off B1383
Car parking: Free
By rail: Audley End
ADDRESS: Audley End
Railway, Audley End
Estate, Bruncketts,
Wendons Ambo, Saffron
Walden, Essex CB11 4JL
TEL: 01799 541354
LENGTH OF LINE:
1.5-mile round trip
OPENING TIMES:
Mar–Oct: 2p.m. every
w/end, public holidays,
and daily during school
summer holidays
FACILITIES: Shop with
light refreshments,
toilets, picnic area
DISABLED: No
wheelchair access to
trains, but good access
elsewhere

SET IN GROUNDS landscaped by Capability Brown and overlooked by Audley End House, a grand Jacobean mansion, this is one of the country's most picturesque 10.25″ gauge miniature railways. Enjoy the round trip through shady woodlands across the River Cam and back, steam hauled every Sunday and most Saturdays. During December the line runs to Santa's Grotto where all children receive a present. In summer, concerts are held in the mansion grounds.

AVON VALLEY

HOW TO FIND US:
By car: Bitton Station is midway between Bath and Bristol on A431
Car parking: Free
By rail/bus: Train to Keynsham, then 1.5mile walk to Bitton Station; Badgerline bus services (phone 0117 955 3231)
By bike: Bristol to Bath Railway Path (Route 4 of the National Cycle Network)

ADDRESS: Bitton Station, Bath Road, Willsbridge, Bristol BS30 6HD
TEL: 0117 932 5538
INFOLINE: 0117 932 7296
WEBSITE: www. avonvalleyrailway.co.uk
LINE LENGTH: 2 miles
OPENING TIMES:
Station and facilities open w/ends and school holidays. Steam trains operate Easter–end Sep: Sun & public holidays, plus Wed in Aug. Phone for details
FACILITIES: Buffet, gift shop and toilets
DISABLED: One coach specially adapted for wheelchairs. Phone in advance. Buffet and shop accessible, no disabled toilets

THE AVON VALLEY RAILWAY is more than just a train ride. Take a trip on a steam train into the scenic heart of the valley; catch a glimpse of the past when steam was king; experience the unique sights, sounds and smells of a bygone age, and see the trains being restored at this working museum dedicated to the glorious days of steam. The standard guage railway runs from Oldland Common, south through Bitton to the River Avon. The Railway also run courses giving enthusiasts the opportunity to drive and fire a steam locomotive. Other attractions include the Avon Valley Country Park and the Avon Wildlife Trust's Willsbridge Mill, plus an extensive network of footpaths, including the Avon Walkway and the Monarchs Way. With many special events organised including Sunday luncheon dining trains, this is the ideal place to come for a family day out.

BARLEYLANDS FARM MUSEUM

HOW TO FIND US:
By car: Just off A129 between Billericay and Wickford, and within 1/2 mile of A127
Car parking: On site
By bus: Thames Premier 100 service (not Sun) or NIBS No 222
ADDRESS: Barleylands Farm Museum, Billericay, Essex CM11 2UD
TEL: 01268 290229
LENGTH OF LINE: 800 yds
OPENING TIMES: Early Mar–mid-Nov: Sun & public holidays, (daily running except Sat during Aug)
FACILITIES: Shop, tea-rooms, restaurant, children's play area, farm museum
DISABLED: Wheelchair access

This 7.25" GAUGE line was opened in 1985 utilising the locomotives, rolling stock and track from the North Benfleet Miniature Railway. The line is normally operated in two sections, Museum to Little Wood junction, where there is a trailing junction to the line from the Boot Fair. The four locomotives from NBMR are one–eighth full size—a 9F, a Britannia, a free lance 2-6-0 and a 4-4-2 tank engine. A further engine, one–third full size, is based on a Hunslet design for the North Wales Narrow Gauge Railway. The railway forms part of Barleylands Farm, with various craft studios, museum and animal centre.

BARROW HILL ROUNDHOUSE

HOW TO FIND US:
By car: 4 miles east of Chesterfield. M1 (Junction 30), take A619 to Staveley, then road to Eckington
Car parking: Free
By rail: Chesterfield
By bus: Stagecoach Nos 56, 80, 90 from Chesterfield bus station
ADDRESS: Barrow Hill Roundhouse, Campbell Drive, Barrow Hill, Staveley, Chesterfield
TEL: 01246 472450
WEBSITE: www. shu.ac.uk/city/ community/bhess
OPENING TIMES: All year 9–5: Sat and Sun
FACILITIES: Light refreshments, museum, souvenir shop
DISABLED: Wheelchair access (phone ahead)

Barrow hill is Britain's last surviving operational roundhouse, providing the experience of seeing locomotives around a covered turntable in a shed that has changed very little since it was built by Midland Railway over 120 years ago. The building is a unique example of 19th–century railway architecture. One of the largest collections of steam, diesel and electric locomotives is now assembled in the Roundhouse, and a main line connection has been established allowing the displays to be varied on a regular basis. Outside, the original yard and sidings are being restored.

BATTLEFIELD

HOW TO FIND US:
By car: Follow the brown tourist signs from the A444, A447 and B585 roads
Car Parking: Large free car park at Shackerstone;narrowboats can visit and moor by Ashby Canal bridge
ADDRESS: Shackerstone Station, Shackerstone, Leics, CV13 6NW
TEL: 01827 880 754
LENGTH OF LINE: 5 miles
OPENING TIMES:
Steam services operate mid-Mar–Nov: w/ends & public holidays
FACILITIES: Tea room, buffet on mosttrains, souvenir shop
DISABLED: Phone ahead

THE BATTLE WAS Bosworth Field, where the bloody Wars of the Roses were settled, and the last king of England to die in battle was slain. You can travel through the scenic countryside from Shackerstone to visit the site and the Battlefield Visitor Centre which tells the story of that momentous day in 1485. Shackerstone Station itself, the headquarters of the standard gauge line, dates from 1873, and houses a fascinating collection of local railway history. Above the Engine Shed is a viewing area overlooking the lines, signal box and Leicestershire countryside.

BEAMISH

HOW TO FIND US:
By car: Follow the signs from the A1(M) Jct 63
Car parking: Free
By rail: Sunderland and Durham City
By bus: Nos 775 and 778 from Sunderland, 720 from Durham,
ADDRESS: Beamish, The North of England Open Air Museum, County Durham DH9 0RG
TEL: 01207 231811
WEBSITE: www.beamish.org.uk
OPENING TIMES:
Open all year from 10–5. Closed Mon and Fri in winter. Check for Xmas opening times
FACILITIES: Tea rooms, souvenir shops, period pub
DISABLED: Limited wheelchair access

THIS VAST 300-acre open air museum recreates life in Northern England in the 1800s and early 1900s. There is an 1867 Railway Station, complete with goods yard, signal box, coal cells, locomotives and rolling stock. The newest exhibit is the 1825 railway, Pockerley Waggonway, which takes visitors on a recreation of the world's first steam-hauled passenger train, headed by the replica of Stephenson's "Locomotion No 1". Nearby, in The Great Engine Shed, is the Engineer's Drawing Office, Engine Driver's Den and a magnificent 1822 locomotive. There is an early 19th–century town, colliery village, working farm and 1.5–mile period tramway.

BEER HEIGHTS

By car: From Exeter, or Lyme Regis follow the A3052 to Beer

Car/coach parking: Free

By rail/bus: Buses run from Axminster, call 01392 382 800

ADDRESS: Beer Heights Light Railway, Pecorama, Beer, Seaton, Devon EX12 3NA

TEL: 01297 21542

WEBSITE: www.peco-uk.com

LENGTH OF LINE: 1-mile

OPENING TIMES:
Mid-Apr–Sep & Oct half-term: 10–5 Mon–Fri; 10–1 Sat; Easter & late-May–Aug: 10–5.30 Sun

FACILITIES: Licensed restaurant, refreshments

DISABLED:
Wheelchair access

SET IN THE Pecorama Pleasure Gardens, this miniature steam- and diesel-driven railway takes you on a fantastic trip over bridges, past gardens and through tunnels to Deepwater Lake. A new zig-zag section leads down an incline to the disused Beer Mine itself (unfortunately, despite the name, this was a source of chalk rather than ale). The gardens boast many other attractions including an indoor display of model railways, an aviary, an assault course, a wooden maze and crazy golf. At Beer itself, there are some delightful shingle beaches where, in summer, you can hire boats.

BIDEFORD RAILWAY MUSEUM

HOW TO FIND US:
By car: Follow the A39. The Museum is at the east end of the old Bideford Bridge

Car parking: Free

By rail: Barnstaple

By bus: Buses between Barnstaple and Bideford stop outside the station

ADDRESS: Bideford Station, Railway Terrace, Bideford, Devon EX39 4BB

TEL: 01237 423585

OPENING TIMES:
All year: 2–5 Sun; Easter–Oct: 2–5 Tue, Thu, Sun & public holidays

FACILITIES:
Refreshments, book shop, souvenir shop

DISABLED:
No wheelchair access

THIS MUSEUM IS housed in the old rebuilt signal box at Bideford station on the former Barnstaple–Torrington line, and displays many fascinating artifacts and items of local railway interest on two floors. Various railway vehicles, including a BR Mk 1 carriage, a brake van, a goods van and an SR PMV parcels van are displayed on a short length of track; there are plans to give rides in the brake van in the near future. More entertainment can be found at Bideford's nearby "Big Sheep" sheep centre, where regular sheep steeplechases (or sheeplechases) are run. The down platform Station building still exists and is used by the Northern Devon Coast and Countryside Service.

BIRMINGHAM RAILWAY MUSEUM

HOW TO FIND US:
By car: On the A41.
Car parking: On site
By rail: Tyseley
By bus: West Midlands
No 37 from city centre
ADDRESS: Birmingham
Railway Museum,
670 Warwick Road,
Tyseley, Birmingham
B11 2HL
TEL: 0121 707 4696
Vintage Trains (as above)
FAX: 0121 764 4645
LENGTH OF LINE: 660 yds
OPENING TIMES:
Static display: 10–5
daily; engines in steam
most weekends; brake
van rides Apr–Oct: 1st
Sun of month
FACILITIES: Souvenir
shop, refreshments,
DISABLED: Phone in
advance

THIS FASCINATING MUSEUM, in a former Great Western Railway/British Rail steam shed, is noted for its education service. It runs guided tours and live presentations, as well as driving experience courses when members of the public can actually drive and fire a steam locomotive. There is a viewinggallery, passenger demonstration line and station, and the museum contains much specialised railway engineering machinery. Tyseley is the centre for "Vintage Trains"; the company runs the "Shakespeare Express" on the fastest regular steam trips between Birmingham Snow Hill, Tyseley and Stratford-Upon-Avon, having been reintroduced in 1999 on Sundays after a lapse of nearly 30 years. This express train route opened in 1908 and much of the original Great Western Railway remains, including double track main line, semaphore signals and original stations.

HOW TO FIND US:
By car: Sheffield Park is
on the A275
Car parking: At
Sheffield Park and
Horsted Keynes
By rail/bus: From East
Grinstead
ADDRESS:
Bluebell Railway,
Sheffield Park Station,
E.Sussex TN22 3QL
TEL: 01825 723777
INFOLINE: 01825 722370
WEBSITE: www.
bluebell-railway.co.uk
LENGTH OF LINE: 9 miles
OPENING TIMES: W/ends
through the year;
May–Sep and school
half terms: daily
FACILITIES: Café, real ale
bar, gift shop, all at
Sheffield Park
DISABLED: Wheelchair
access and adapted
toilets. A recently
restored coach with
wheelchair lift facilities
is available on certain
days of operation

THE BLUEBELL LINE, perhaps the country's most famous railway, winds its way through over a century of railway tradition. The headquarters at Sheffield Park is home to the region's largest locomotive collection (over 30 steam locomotives and more than 100 carriages and wagons), as well as a museum of railway memorabilia and a reconstructed signal box. Take a walk around the engine shed and see the magnificent locomotives at close quarters. At Horsted Keynes, possibly the finest preserved station in the country, there is an award-winning carriage and wagon display. Every last detail has been meticulously researched, from the elegant fittings in the sumptuous Pullman dining cars to the period advertisements that adorn the station walls. The staff here are also responsible for maintaining the rolling stock, as well as restoring old carriages. Horsted Keynes is home of a popular Steam Fair and Vintage Vehicle Rally each July. In spring the trains run through the fields of bluebells which give the line its name.

BODMIN & WENFORD

HOW TO FIND US:
By car: Station is on the B3268
Car parking: Only at Bodmin General
By rail: Bodmin Parkway
By bus: Call
01208 798 898
ADDRESS: Bodmin General Station, Bodmin, Cornwall PL31 1AQ
TEL: 01208 73666
WEBSITE: www. members.aol.com/ bodwenf
LENGTH OF LINE:
6.5 miles
OPENING TIMES:
Jun–Sep: daily ;
Mar–May and Oct: selected days
FACILITIES: Buffet and souvenir shop
DISABLED:
Limited access

Two lines run from the railway's headquarters at Bodmin General, a restored Great Western Railway station, both affording ample opportunity for picnics, walks and exploration of the Cornish countryside. A recently re-opened stretch of track leads to Boscarne Junction, the starting point for the "Camel Trail" – a popular foot and cycle path – while at Colesloggett Halt, on the line to Bodmin Parkway, a footpath leads to the nature trails and cycle tracks of Cardinham Woods. At Bodmin Parkway itself, you can take a scenic walk along to Lanhydrock, a National Trust property.

BOWES

HOW TO FIND US:
By car: Springwell is near Gateshead, just off the B1288
Car parking: Free
By rail: Gateshead
By bus: 184 & 189 from Washington and 187 & 188 from Gateshead
ADDRESS: Bowes Railway, Springwell Village, Gateshead NE9 7QJ
TEL: 0191 416 1847
WEBSITE: www. bowesrailway.co.uk
LENGTH OF LINE:
1.25 miles
OPENING TIMES:
Static visits: 9–4 Mon–Fri; phone for operating days
FACILITIES:
Souvenir shop, café
DISABLED:
Wheelchair access

Developed to carry coal from the mines of northwest Durham to the River Tyne at Jarrow, the Bowes Railway affords a fascinating insight into the area's great industrial heritage. Steam locomotives pull traditional colliery break vans from the museum centre to Blackham's Hill where you can view two working inclines. Designed by George Stephenson in 1826, these are the only preserved standard gauge rope-hauled inclines in the world. A superb collection of colliery wagons is complemented by some magnificent mid-Victorian stone buildings, including a chain-maker's, blacksmith's, wagon and tub shops.

BREDGAR & WORMSHILL

HOW TO FIND US:
By Car: Leave M20 at
junction 8, follow A20,
turn left onto B2163,
The Warren is 4 miles
beyond Hollingbourne
Car parking: Available
By rail: Hollingbourne
(no connecting buses)
ADDRESS: The Bredgar
& Wormshill Light
Railway, The Warren,
Bredgar, Sittingbourne,
Kent ME9 8AT
TEL: 01622 884254
FAX: 01622 884668
OPENING TIMES: May–
Sep: 1st Sun in month;
groups by arrangement;
FACILITIES: Light
refreshments at Warren
Wood Station
DISABLED: Call ahead

THIS PRIVATELY OWNED, fully operational, narrow gauge railway has a fine collection of steam locomotives from all over the world. Describing itself as a charming eccentricity, there are stations, waiting rooms and signal boxes built with an eye for 1920s' style. On open days there is a regular steam service on the half-mile line between Warren Wood and Stony Shaw through attractive Kent country-side. As well as unlimited rides on vintage trains, there are woodland walks, picnic sites and a large locomotive shed to explore. There is also a collection of steam road and agricultural machines and a Bean car collection.

BRESSINGHAM STEAM MUSEUM

HOW TO FIND US:
By Car: Just off the
A1066, 2 miles west of
Diss
Car parking: Free
By rail: Diss
ADDRESS: Diss, Norfolk
IP22 2AB
TEL: 01379 687 386
24-HOUR INFOLINE:
01379 687 682
WEBSITE: www.
bressingham.co.uk
LENGTH OF LINE: 5 miles
OPENING TIMES:
Apr–Oct: daily; special
events; Xmas Specials
FACILITIES: Souvenir
shop, café, gardens and
plant centre
DISABLED: Wheelchair
access; limited number
of wheelchairs; adapted
toilets

BRESSINGHAM OFFERS AN unparalleled array of steam attractions set in six acres of enchanting gardens. There are no fewer than three narrow gauge lines – the Nursery Railway, which passes the nearby lake and woodland and gives views of the splendid Roydon church; the Waveney Valley line, running over watermeadows and through rhododendron banks; and the Garden Railway. The extensive collection of standard gauge locomotives is complemented by traction engines, steam wagons, stationary engines and "The Gallopers", a magnificent Victorian steam carousel. Another attraction is the National "Dad's Army" Collection.

HOW TO FIND US:
By car: Just off the A41 between Aylesbury and Bicester

Car parking: Free at Quinton Road

By rail: Aylesbury

ADDRESS: Quainton Road Station, Quainton, Aylesbury, Bucks HP22 4BY

TEL: 01296 655720

INFOLINE: 01296 655450

LENGTH OF LINE:
2.5 miles

OPENING TIMES:
Apr–Oct: Sun & public holidays; Jul–Aug: Wed

FACILITIES: Gift and book shop, second-hand bookshop, refreshments

DISABLED:
Wheelchair access and adapted toilets

THE BEAUTIFULLY PRESERVED Victorian station at Quainton Road, which houses the Buckinghamshire Railway Centre, was once a stop on the Metropolitan & Great Central line from Baker Street to Verney Junction. It holds a huge collection of locomotives, carriages and wagons along with railway memorabilia from all over the world. As well as full-sized steam train rides, you can take a trip on the exquisitely crafted tiny locomotives that chug around its miniature railway. The centre organises various events throughout the year, including , regular "Day Out with Thomas" events.

BURE VALLEY

HOW TO FIND US:
By car: A140 or A1151

Car parking: Free at Wroxham and Aylsham

By rail: Wroxham

By bus: From Aylsham and Wroxham

TEL: 01263 733 858

WEBSITE: www.bvrw.co.uk

LENGTH OF LINE: 9 miles

OPENING TIMES:
Easter–late Oct

FACILITIES:
Café, picnic area, shop

DISABLED:
Wheelchair access at both main stations and wheelchair accessible coaches

FIVE STEAM LOCOMOTIVES operate on this 15" gauge line, Norfolk's longest narrow gauge railway, transporting passengers in luxurious upholstered coaches. The journey begins in the old market town of Aylsham, where there are workshops, a small museum and a model railway, and finishes at Wroxham, "The Capital of the Broads" – combined train and boat excursions are available. There are Steam Locomotive Driver Training Courses available during off peak periods.

CADEBY

Tʜᴇ ᴄᴀᴅᴇʙʏ ʟɪɢʜᴛ ʀᴀɪʟᴡᴀʏ was founded by the late Reverend Teddy Boston, the original "Fat Controller" of the Thomas the Tank Engine books, and is one of the smallest full-size passenger railways in the world. It is also home to other attractions such as a large model railway, a miniature 5" gauge passenger-carrying line and a "Fiery Elias", a Foster agricultural engine. There is a brass-rubbing centre in the nearby 13th-century church of All Saints. The railway hosts special events throughout the year including a Morris Dance Day in May and a Teddy Bears' Picnic in June.

CHASEWATER

Cʜᴀsᴇᴡᴀᴛᴇʀ ʀᴀɪʟᴡᴀʏ ᴡᴀs built in the 1870s to speed up the transport of coal from the Cannock Chase coalfield to the hungry Black Country industries – it had previously been transported by canal. Today you can take a ride from Brownhills West, where there is a display of engines and carriages, across a quarter-mile-long causeway to Norton Lakeside. This adjoins the Norton Wildfowl Reserve, home to various species of local wildlife, including 18 types of dragonfly. A 572yd extension to a new station at Chasewater Heaths will open during 2001, and work is also proceeding on a two-mile extension to Chasetown.

CHINNOR & PRINCES RISBOROUGH

HOW TO FIND US:
By car: Chinnor is on the B4009 between Princes Risborough and Junction 6 of the M40
Car parking: Free on site
By rail: Princes Risborough
ADDRESS: Chinnor and Princes Risborough Railway Co, Chinnor Station, Station Road, Chinnor, Oxfordshire OX9 4ER
INFOLINE: 01844 353535
LENGTH OF LINE: 4 miles
OPENING TIMES:
Easter–Oct: w/ends; Santa and Mince Pie specials in Dec
FACILITIES: Souvenir shop, on-train buffet, picnic area
DISABLED: Call ahead

THE CHINNOR AND PRINCES RISBOROUGH Railway Association was formed in 1989 to restore part of the disused Watlington branch or "Icknield Line". Every weekend visitors take a round trip through four miles of charming countryside from Oxfordshire into Buckinghamshire. The Association owns seven locomotives, the oldest built in 1916, and there are regular visits by "guest" engines from around the country. Other attractions in the area include Rycote, a 15th-century chapel, and Thame, an unspoilt village where medieval timber frame buildings stand next to stately Georgian town houses.

CHOLSEY & WALLINGFORD

HOW TO FIND US:
By car: Wallingford is on the River Thames, A4130 by road
Car parking: Ample parking
By rail: Cholsey
ADDRESS: Cholsey & Wallingford Railway, St Johns Road, Wallingford, Oxon
TEL: 01491 652295
FAX: 01491 651696
INFOLINE: 01491 835067
LENGTH OF LINE:
2.5 miles
OPENING TIMES:
trains operate: Easter–Oct last w/end of each month; phone for special events
FACILITIES: Café, shop at Wallingford
DISABLED: Call ahead

THIS RESTORED LINE, part of the old Great Western Railway, takes its passengers on a ride through the leafy Oxfordshire countryside. The line was originally opened in 1866, and is one of the oldest surviving GWR lines in the Thames Valley. The station museum at Wallingford has a collection of local railway memorabilia and a model of the original station (about 1930) with an 'N' gauge model railway. 15 minutes walk away, on the banks of the River Thames, is the town of Wallingford, one of the oldest chartered towns in the country. From the station at Cholsey, visit St Mary's Church where Agatha Christie is buried (another 15-minute walk).

CHURNET VALLEY

HOW TO FIND US:
By car: On the A520
Car parking: Opposite
the station
By rail: Stoke-on-Trent
or Blythe Bridge stations
ADDRESS: Cheddleton
Station, Cheddleton,
Staffordshire Moor-
lands, ST13 7EE
TEL: 01538 360522
WEBSITE: www.
dacer.force9.co.uk
OPENING TIMES:
Steam trains: late
Mar–early Oct, Sun &
public holidays;
Aug: every Wed
LENGTH OF LINE:
6.5-mile round trip
FACILITIES: Picnic island,
tea rooms, gift shop
DISABLED: Wheelchair
access; train rides by
arrangement

IN THE HEART of the Staffordshire moor-
lands, the Churnet Valley Railway aims to
recreate the atmosphere and ambience of a
1950s steam-operated country line. The line
is gradually being restored and reopened to
the public. Currently it runs from the hand-
some Victorian station at Cheddleton
through one of the longest tunnels on
Britain's preserved railways to the beautiful
"Hidden Valley" at Consall. Cheddleton's
famous flint museum, with its collection of
17th- and 18th-century watermills, is just a
short walk away.

CLEETHORPES COAST

HOW TO FIND US:
By car: Lakeside is on
the Cleethorpes resort
road
Car parking: On site
By rail: Cleethorpes
By bus: No.17
ADDRESS:
Cleethorpes Coast Light
Railway Ltd, Kings
Road, Cleethorpes,
Lincs DN35 0AG
TEL: 01472 604657
OPENING TIMES:
All year: w/ends;
Good Fri–Sept: daily
FACILITIES: Tea rooms at
Lakeside, souvenir shop
at Kingsway Station
DISABLED: Wheelchair
access to stations

THIS FRIENDLY, FAMILY-RUN 15" gauge steam
railway is the only one of its kind left
in Lincolnshire. Coasting along from
Kingsway to Lakeside, it offers jolly little
trips around and through the local scenery;
on one side is the holiday fun of Lakeside
Park, on the other the varied wildlife and
busy shipping lanes of the Humber Estuary.
Nearby attractions include Cleethorpes'
ancient church, Discovery Centre and The
Jungle (Tropical World).

COLNE VALLEY

HOW TO FIND US:
By car: NW of Braintree on A1017
Car parking: On site
By rail: Braintree
By bus: No. 88/89
ADDRESS: Yeldham Road, Castle Hedingham, Essex CO9 3DZ
TEL: 01787 461174
WEBSITE: www.cvr.org.uk
LENGTH OF LINE: 1 mile
OPENING TIMES:
Mar–Dec: 11–5 (dusk if earlier) (phone for free timetable)
FACILITIES: Buffet, picnic area, farm park (rare, tradional and modern farm animals), Pullman restaurant train
DISABLED:
Wheelchair access to most of the site

A HIGHLY SUCCESSFUL reconstruction of a typical Essex country branch line, this attractive railway on the banks of the River Colne now carries as many passengers per year as it did in its heyday. Part of its success is due to its promotion of luxury travel. The opulent ambience of the Orient Express is evoked on its Pullman train, featuring beautifully restored coaches (all meals in these carriages must be pre-booked). Steam and heritage diesel trains offer rides on Sundays and certain mid-week days in summer holidays. There is free admission to the Farm Park.

DARLINGTON MUSEUM

HOW TO FIND US:
By car: North of Darlington town centre
Car parking: Free on site
By rail: Darlington North
ADDRESS:
North Road Station, Darlington DL3 6ST
TEL: 01325 460532
OPENING TIMES:
Daily: 10–5, closed throughout Jan
FACILITIES:
Refreshment area, gift and book shop
DISABLED:
Wheelchair access, parking facilities

D ARLINGTON IS ONE of the great names of railway history. The Stockton and Darlington Railway was opened in 1825 by George Stephenson's 'Locomotion'—the locomotive that pulled the world's first passenger train. Stephenson also surveyed the route and was the company's first engineer. The Locomotion is just one of the exhibits in the centre's remarkable collection of engines, carriages and wagons. There is also a large model railway and, in the Locomotive Works, you can see a new Pacific locomotive being built. Steam train rides over a short length of line are available on special days.

HOW TO FIND US:
By car: Lydney is on the B4234, signposted off A48
Car parking: Free car park at Norchard
By rail: Lydney Junction
ADDRESS: Dean Forest Railway Co. Ltd, Forest Road, Lydney, Glos GL15 4ET
TEL: (shop) 01594 845840
INFOLINE: 01594 843423
WEBSITE: www.deanforestrailway.co.uk
LENGTH OF LINE: 2 miles
OPENING TIMES:
Apr, May, Sep: Sun; Jun, Jul: Wed, Sun; Aug: Thu, Sat, Sun
FACILITIES: Shop at Norchard, picnic area, refreshments available on operational days
DISABLED: Wheelchair access to both museum and trains

THE ROYAL FOREST of Dean, one of Britain's best-loved forests, a hilly woodland of ponds, streams and stepping stones, is full of secrets from the past, well worth exploring. Old maps are are criss-crossed with the tramroads and railways built to carry the minerals once mined here. Dean Forest Railway, dating back to 1809, is the last remnant of the "Severn and Wye Railway" system. The line currently runs two miles south to the mainline station at Lydney Junction from the headquarters at Norchard Railway Centre, where there is also a museum with an old telephone exchange and a collection of railway memorabilia. The line boasts five level crossings, three of which are manually operated. An historic parish church is served by St Mary's Halt, with an adjacent park and lake. The Dean Forest Railway Society is currently upgrading a two-mile extension to Parkend Village in the forest (last passenger traffic on the line was in 1928). This is no isolated beauty spot, however. For centuries the livelihoods of many people have depended on their ability to work the forest and you can find out more about the living history of the area at the Dean Heritage Centre where there is a recreated forester's cottage, a water wheel and a beam engine.

DERBY INDUSTRIAL MUSEUM

HOW TO FIND US:
By car: City centre
Car parking: Local parking only
By rail: Derby
ADDRESS: Derby Industrial Museum, Full Street, Derby, DE1 3AR
TEL: 01332 255308
OPENING TIMES: 11–5 Mon, 10–5 Tue–Sat, 2–5 Sun & public holidays
FACILITIES: Museum shop, baby-changing facilities
DISABLED: Wheelchair access; parking by prior arrangement

Housed in a former silk mill, this museum has collected a vast range of exhibits designed to illustrate Derby's industrial heritage. The entire history of the technical age is represented, from George Fletcher's 1850 beam engine to the Rolls-Royce RB211 Turbofan aeroplane engine – the museum has the finest collection of Rolls-Royce aero engines in the world. The story of the Midland railway industry and its effect on Derby is told in the Railway Galleries, where there is a model railway, a replica signal box and, for those interested in the future of railways rather than simply preserving the past, a Railway Research Centre which looks at the possible form and uses of the railways of tomorrow.

DERWENT VALLEY

HOW TO FIND US:
By car: Off the A166 Bridlington road
Car parking: free
By rail/bus: York. York Station to Stamford Bridge bus service stops at park
ADDRESS: Derwent Valley Light Railway, Murton Park, Murton Lane, York YO1 3UF
TEL: 01904 489966
LENGTH OF LINE: 0.5 miles
OPENING TIMES: Park open daily Feb–Oct. The railway runs Easter–Sep: Sun and public holidays; Dec for Santa Specials
FACILITIES: Refreshments, gift shop
DISABLED: some wheelchair access

The delightful Murton Park, three miles east of York, is home to a Museum of Farming, which contains various ancient and rather dangerous looking pieces of farming equipment; an ersatz Dark Age Settlement where you can wander through reconstructed wattle and daub huts; a small maze; various picnic and play areas; and, of course, the Derwent Valley Light Railway. Formerly known as the Blackberry Line, this opened in 1993 and trips its way through half a mile of pleasant Yorkshire countryside. The railway has a large collection of locomotives and a restored signal box as well as various items of rolling stock.

DEVON RAILWAY CENTRE

HOW TO FIND US:
By car: 10 minutes from
Exeter, 4 miles from
Tiverton on the A396
Car parking: On site
By rail: Exeter
By bus: 55 and 55A

ADDRESS: Devon
Railway Centre,
Bickleigh, near Tiverton,
Devon EX16 8RG

TEL: 01884 855671

LENGTH OF LINE: 0.5 miles

OPENING TIMES:
Easter–May: Sun &
public holidays;
Jun–Oct: Wed–Fri, Sun;
Nov, Dec: Sun; school
holidays: Sun–Fri

FACILITIES:
Refreshments, souvenir
shop, picnic area

DISABLED: Some
wheelchair access

THE DEVON RAILWAY CENTRE is located in the picturesque village of Bickleigh. The lovingly restored Great Western station dates from 1885. A 2' narrow gauge line has been laid on which visitors are taken through the beautiful Exe Valley to the centre's riverside picnic area. There is also a recently opened museum with a large collection of narrow gauge equipment, including eight locomotives and a Royal coach dating from c1880. The stationary engines are all maintained in working order. Alongside the original station are two full-size coaches containing some of the best model railways in Britain.

DIDCOT RAILWAY CENTRE

HOW TO FIND US:
By car: On the A4130
By rail: Didcot Parkway
By bus: Stagecoach
and Oxford and Thames
Travel

ADDRESS: Great Western
Society Ltd, Didcot
Railway Centre, Didcot,
Oxon, OX11 7NJ

TEL: 01235 817200

WEBSITE: www.
didcotrailwaycentre.
org.uk

LENGTH OF LINE:
1,000 yds

OPENING TIMES:
All year: w/ends;
Apr–Sep and school
holidays: daily

FACILITIES: Gift shop,
refreshments, picnic area

DISABLED: Steps at subway entrance, call in advance for wheelchair assistance

DESIGNED AND ENGINEERED by Isambard Kingdom Brunel, the Great Western Railway ran from Bristol to London for over a century. Today it is recreated and celebrated at this living museum in Didcot, the focus of which is the engine shed, with a collection of over 20 steam locomotives. A reproduction of the broad gauge 1839 Firefly is currently being built in the Locomotive Works. There is also a recreation of a typical branch line and country station as well as regular signalling demonstrations and "Steamdays", including special Travelling Post Office days when you can find out how mailbags used to be exchanged at speed.

EAST ANGLIA TRANSPORT MUSEUM

29

HOW TO FIND US:
By car: Off the A12 and A146
Car parking: adjacent
By rail: Oulton Broad
By bus: Nos L11, L12, L18, L19
ADDRESS: Chapel Road, Carlton Colville, Lowestoft, Suffolk NR33 8BL
TEL: 01502 518459
LENGTH OF LINE: 300 yds
OPENING TIMES:
Sun and bank holidays May–Sep; Wed and Sat from June–Sep; every w/day from end of July–1st Sept
FACILITIES: Picnic areas, café and gift shop
DISABLED: Toilets, Wheelchair access to trains

This is home to the East Suffolk Light Railway, a 2' gauge line which wends its way through some of the three acres of woodland surrounding the museum. The railway began operating in 1973 and is a passenger-carrying light railway – many of its features, including the track, signals and signal box, were rescued from discontinued lines elsewhere in the country. There are 2 diesel locomotives, No 2 is a Simplex motorail type 2DL built in 1934 and No 4 built in 1936. The museum itself contains a reconstructed 1930s street scene with working trams, and trolleybuses. Many other types of vehicle are also on show.

EAST ANGLIAN RAILWAY MUSEUM

HOW TO FIND US:
By car: Off A1124 and A134, near Colchester
Car parking: On site
By rail: Chappel (Great Eastern service from Mark's Tey to Sudbury)
By bus: Colchester–Halstead Nos 88 & 88c (Sun)
ADDRESS: East Anglian Railway Museum, Chappel & Wakes Colne Station, Nr Colchester, Essex CO6 2DS
TEL: 01206 242524
WEBSITE: http://www.binternet.com/~earm/
LENGTH OF LINE: 0.5 miles
OPENING TIMES:
10–5 daily. Phone for details of steam events
FACILITIES: Bookshop, buffet, picnic area
DISABLED: Toilets

Situated next to the spectacular Chappel viaduct, this museum has a wide collection of locomotives and rolling stock, some undergoing restoration and repair in the specially built Restoration Shed. There are three working signal boxes on the site, as well as a signalling display near the miniature railway, with its own booking office and Locomotive Shed. Dating from the 1890s, the station buildings are splendid examples of railway architecture. Underneath the station, in what were storage arches, is a visitor centre with a display showing the history of the Stour Valley line and of the museum. Another attraction is the restored Goods Shed, originally used to handle freight.

EAST KENT

THE ORIGINAL EAST KENT RAILWAY was built early this century to serve the area's collieries. It was one of several lines across the country engineered and run by Colonel H F Stephens in his own distinctive style – *i.e.* cheaply. He used antiquated locomotives and stock, and the lines were characterised by steep inclines and sharp curves. The museum at Shepherdswell, the railway's current headquarters, tells the story of the line and this interesting character. The station itself is a re-creation of the one which stood here until the 1950s.

EAST LANCASHIRE

A WIDE RANGE of lovingly restored steam and diesel locomotives carry passengers between the five scenic towns on this line. There are plenty of attractions to be found along the way including Irwell Vale's colourful gardens, the Victorian mill at Summerseat, the Heritage Centre at Ramsbottom and the art galleries, museums and dry ski slope at Bury. Opposite Bolton Street Station is the Bury Transport Museum with a collection of road and rail vehicles used during the past 100 years, a collection of railway signs, and a display of photographs of the present East Lancashire Railway. The railway also operates Friday evening dinner trains.

EAST SOMERSET

HOW TO FIND US:
By car: Just off A361
By rail: Frome
By bus: From
Shepton Mallet
ADDRESS: Cranmore
Railway Station,
Shepton Mallet,
Somerset BA4 4QP
TEL: 01749 880417
WEBSITE: www.
soft.net.uk/carver
LENGTH OF LINE: 3 miles
OPENING TIMES:
Trains run Jan–Mar &
Nov: Sun; Apr, May &
Oct: Sat, Sun;
Jun & Sep: Wed–Sun;
Jul–Aug: daily
FACILITIES:
Licensed restaurant, art
gallery, video coach,
playground
DISABLED: Wheelchair
access

ONE OF ONLY two remaining all-steam railways in the country, it was founded in 1974 by the artist David Shepherd on the site of the original East Somerset Railway or "Strawberry Line" which first started operating in 1858. There is a fine replica Victorian Engine Shed where some of the country's most famous locomotives are housed including "Black Prince", "Green Knight" and an 1877 tank engine. There is also a nature reserve and art gallery where prints of Mr Shepherd's works are displayed. The nearby Cranmore Tower, a 19th-century folly, affords good views of the surrounding countryside.

EASTBOURNE

HOW TO FIND US:
By car: A22 towards
Eastbourne
Car parking: On-site
By rail: Eastbourne
By bus: Call 01323 416
416
Address: EMSR,
Lottbridge Drove,
Eastbourne,
East Sussex BN23 6NS
TEL: 01323 520229
WEBSITE: www.
emsr.co.uk
LENGTH OF LINE:
Nearly 1 mile
OPENING TIMES:
Apr–Sep & Autumn half
term: 10–5 daily;
Oct: w/ends
FACILITIES: Café, picnic
areas, souvenir/gift
shop
DISABLED: Limited
wheelchair access

LOVINGLY BUILT AND operated by Mike and Rachel Wadey, this miniature steam railway (1/8th scale) hauls its passengers around the five acres of Southbourne lake, passing through Padgham Tunnel and over Southbourne Crossing on the way. Also on show are a model railway, a garden railway and a locomotive display. For younger visitors there's an adventure playground, nature walk and maze. Special events are run throughout the year and include Easter Sunday, Hornby Roadshow, Vintage and Classic Vehicle Show and a Day Out with Thomas.

EASTLEIGH LAKESIDE

HOW TO FIND US:
By car: M27 Jct 5, take
A335 towards Eastleigh
Car parking: On site
By rail: Southampton
Airport station
ADDRESS: Eastleigh
Lakeside Railway,
Lakeside Country Park,
Wide Lane, Eastleigh,
Hampshire
TEL: 02380 636612
WEBSITE: www.
steamtrain.co.uk
LENGTH OF LINE:
1.25 miles
OPENING TIMES: Every
Sun throughout the year
and daily during school
holidays
FACILITIES: Refresh-
ments, souvenir shop
DISABLED: No wheelchair
access onto carriages,
good access elsewhere

THIS DUAL GAUGE (10.25" and 7.25") railway runs from Eastleigh Parkway through delightfully leafy countryside to Monks Brook Halt – the journey takes a little over 20 minutes. It has a fascinating collection of locomotives including a 1932 model which makes appearances as "Gordon" in "Day out with Thomas" events, a 1947 locomotive built for display in a glass case and run for the first time in 1989, three 10.25" gauge locos on loan and, as a concession to modernity, a miniature replica of the Eurostar Power Car built by a group of students from Southampton University as a project for their degree course.

ELSECAR HERITAGE CENTRE

HOW TO FIND US:
By car: M1 Jct 36,
follow brown tourist
signs along A6135
Car parking: Free
By rail: Barnsley
ADDRESS:
Wath Road, Elsecar,
Barnsley S74 8HJ
TEL: 01266 740203
LENGTH OF LINE: 1 mile
OPENING TIMES:
10–5 daily
FACILITIES:
Refreshments
DISABLED:
Full wheelchair access
and disabled toilets

THE CENTRE'S FULL-SIZED steam railway is just one of a range of exhibits designed to illustrate the industrial history of this area. There is also an interactive science centre; a history centre, where you can try on a variety of Victorian costumes; and over 25 craft workshops making everything from candles to dolls' house furniture. The muse-um's showpiece exhibit is the world-famous Newcomen Beam Engine, built in 1795 to pump water from the local mines. The rail-way itself runs on Sundays alongside the Dearne and Dove Canals which were once used to convey iron and coal to and from the workshops.

EMBSAY & BOLTON

HOW TO FIND US:
By car: Just off the A59
Car parking: On site
By rail: Skipton or Ilkley
By bus: Skipton
ADDRESS: Bolton Abbey
Station, Skipton, North
Yorks BD23 6AF
TEL: 01756 710614
INFOLINE: 01756 795189
WEBSITE: www.
embsayboltonabbey
railway.org.uk
LENGTH OF LINE: 4.5 miles
OPENING TIMES:
Sun through the year,
Sat in June and Sept,
daily from mid Jul–Aug
FACILITIES: Bolton Abbey
Station: Gift shop,
refreshment rooms.
Embsay: Café, gift and
bookshop, picnic area
DISABLED: Wheelchair
access

A TRIP ABOARD this jaunty little steam railway is a great way of exploring the craggy limestone landscape that inspired the Romantic visions of Wordsworth and Turner. Embsay Station, built in 1888, is home to an extensive collection of tank engines. From here you can travel through the North Yorkshire countryside to the reconstructed Bolton Abbey Station. Bolton Abbey, home to the rare Bee Orchid, provides a good base for exploring 75 miles of footpaths through some truly dramatic scenery. Other attractions include the 12th-century priory and fortified Barden Tower.

EXMOOR

HOW TO FIND US:
By car: Bratton Fleming
is just off the A399
Car parking: Free
By rail/bus: Barnstaple
ADDRESS:
Cape of Good Hope
Farm, Bratton Fleming,
Barnstaple, North
Devon EX32 7JN
TEL: 01598 710711
LENGTH OF LINE: 2 miles
OPENING TIMES:
Phone for details
FACILITIES: Teas, light
lunches, gift shop, play
area
DISABLED: Wheelchair
access but not easily to
trains; phone for
assistance

T HIS FRIENDLY, FAMILY-RUN narrow gauge railway is is situated on the edge of the National Park, with wonderful views over Moules Chamber. It has a delightful setting, near the sleepy rural village of Bratton Fleming where half-size specially built steam trains wind their way through two miles of lovely Devon countryside. The railway is just a few miles away from Exmoor Zoological Park, home to a variety of rare and endangered animals; and Arlington Court which contains a wonderful collection of Victorian curios.

FOXFIELD

HOW TO FIND US:
By car: At Blythe
Bridge, off the A50
Car parking: Car park
at Blythe Bridge
By rail: Blythe Bridge
ADDRESS:
Foxfield Steam Railway,
P.O. Box 1967,
Blythe Bridge, Stoke-
on-Trent ST4 8YT
TEL: 01782 396210
WEBSITE: www.
foxfieldrailway.co.uk
LENGTH OF LINE:
2.5 miles
OPENING TIMES:
Trains operate Apr–Sep:
Sun & public holidays
FACILITIES:
Refreshments and
souvenir shop; special
events
DISABLED:
Wheelchair access

IN THE HEART of the Potteries; the ride may not be quite as delicate and refined as a Wedgwood tea service but, in its own way, is just as enjoyable. Built in 1893 to connect a colliery with the national rail system, today the Foxfield Steam Railway provides a pleasant 5-mile round trip through scenic Staffordshire countryside. There's also a standing collection of 20 locomotives and rolling stock. The visitor centres of the Royal Doulton, Spode and Wedgwood factories, where you can see potters crafting the still greatly revered (and greatly expensive) fine china, are all within a few miles' radius.

GARTELL

HOW TO FIND US:
By car: Off A357 just
south of Templecombe
Car parking: Free
By rail: Templecombe
ADDRESS: Common
Lane, Yenston,
Templecombe,
Somerset BA8 0NB
TEL: 01963 370752
LENGTH OF LINE:
0.75 miles
OPENING TIMES:
May–Oct: public holi-
days and certain Sun.
Please phone for details
FACILITIES: Buffet,
souvenir shop, railway
museum, visitor centre,
lakeside picnic area
DISABLED: Wheelchair
access to station and
buffet; one coach
specially adapted to
accommodate a visitor
in a wheelchair

THE GARTELL LIGHT RAILWAY is a family-owned and run 2' gauge line, part of which runs along the trackbed of the old Somerset & Dorset Joint Railway, through the beautiful Blackmore Vale countryside. Sharp curves and gradients as steep as 1 in 30 are a feature of the line, which is fully signalled using a variety of semaphore and colour light signals controlled by two fully operational signal boxes. Normally, an intensive three-train service is operated, using steam and diesel traction, with departures every 15 minutes from the terminus at Templecombe.

HOW TO FIND US:
By car: Toddington is
on the A46
Car parking: On site
By rail: Toddington
By bus: call
01242 602949
ADDRESS: The Railway
Station, Toddington,
Glos GL54 5DT
TEL: 01242 621405
WEBSITE: www.
gwsr.plc.uk
LENGTH OF LINE:
6.5 miles
OPENING TIMES: W/ends
& public holidays, plus
Tue, Wed, Thu in school
holidays
FACILITIES: Book and
gift shop, tearoom,
buffet cars
DISABLED:
Wheelchair access

THE GWR OR "Friendly Line" once formed part of the Great Western route from Birmingham to Cheltenham. Trains currently operate from Toddington to Gotherington, although the line is being extended southwards to Cheltenham. The journey through the Cotswolds provides some superb views of the Malvern Hills and faraway Welsh mountains beyond the Vale of Evesham, as well as a trip through the 693-yard Greet Tunnel. The prestigious "City of Truro" and "Flying Scotsman" locomotives have, in recent years, paid visits to the line.

GREAT COCKROW

HOW TO FIND US:
By car: Take Jct 11 off
the M25, then
follow the A320; the
Railway is 0.5 miles
from St Peter's
Hospital at Chertsey
Car parking: On site
By rail: Chertsey
ADDRESS: Great
Cockrow Railway,
Hardwick Lane,
Lyme, Chertsey
Surrey
TEL: Mon–Fri:
01932 255500,
Sun: 01932 565474
LENGTH OF LINE:
Nearly 2 miles
OPENING TIMES:
May–Oct: Sun
FACILITIES: Café
DISABLED:
Wheelchair access

A MINIATURE RAILWAY that takes itself very seriously, the Great Cockrow offers authentic operation and full signalling with strict block working over nearly two miles of track. Thus it caters for both the serious railway enthusiast and the more casual visitor. There are two routes – the Green takes in the Greywood Tunnel and the "wild" animals of Jungle Halt, whilst the Red traverses a 45-ft viaduct. The twice-daily "Gladesman", the flagship train, covers both the Red and Green routes in a single journey, as does the occasional "Burwood Belle".

HOW TO FIND US:
By car: The Station is just off the A6
Car parking: Ample roadside parking
By rail: Loughborough
By bus: Services run by Midland Fox, call 0116 251 1411
ADDRESS: Great Central Road, Loughborough, Leics LE11 1RW
TEL: 01509 230726
WEBSITE: www. gcrailway.co.uk
LENGTH OF LINE: 8 miles
OPENING TIMES:
All year: w/ends;
May–Sep: daily
FACILITIES: Café, gift shop, buffet cars
DISABLED: Wheelchair access at Quorn and Rothley; specially adapted carriage for

THE GREAT CENTRAL RAILWAY, once part of a network that ran from Manchester to Marylebone, operates Britain's only double track main line steam railway, aiming to recreate the experience of main line rail travel during the heyday of steam locomotives. The northern terminus is the wonderfully preserved Loughborough Central Station, built in 1897. Beneath the booking hall is a museum of railway artifacts. The Engine Shed houses a large fleet of restored locomotives. From here, the journey takes in Quorn and Woodhouse Station with restored World War II buildings, and passes through scenic woodland before crossing Swithland Reservoir via brick and steel viaducts. Swithland Sidings is a restored marshalling yard. The trains also visit Rothley, another beautifully restored, gas-lit country station, before terminating at Leicester North Station.

HOLLYBUSH

HOW TO FIND US:
By car: On the A462
(M6 Jct 11), follow
Brown signs
Car parking: Free
By rail: Landywood,
3 miles away at Great
Wyrley
ADDRESS: Hollybush
Garden Centre &
Aquaria, Warstone Road,
Shareshill, Cannock,
Staffs WV10 7LX
TEL: 01922 418050
WEBSITE: www.
hollybush-garden.com
LENGTH OF LINE: 1 mile
OPENING TIMES:
Apr–Sep: Fri–Wed;
steam trains run Sun
and bank holidays
FACILITIES: Restaurant
and tearoom
DISABLED: Access to the
centre and train platform

A DELIGHTFUL 7.25" gauge miniature railway that jogs its way around Cannock's award-winning Hollybush Garden Centre and its associated nature reserve, home to deer, swans, geese and even wallabies. The carriages are pulled by both diesel and steam locomotives, and there are various examples of scaled replica railway equipment, including some exquisitely rendered miniature signals. The centre itself houses one of the largest collections of fish in the country, with over 240 tanks displaying everything from guppy to piranha.

INSTOW SIGNAL BOX

HOW TO FIND US:
By car: 1.5 miles from
the Torridge Bridge on
the North Devon Link
Road. The Box is on
the sea front
Car parking: Free
By bus: Buses from
Appledore, Bideford,
Barnstaple, Exeter,
Ilfracombe, Okehampton and Westwood Ho!
ADDRESS: Bideford &
Instow Railway Group,
Bideford Station, Railway Terrace, Bideford,
Devon EX39 4BB
TEL: 01237 423585
OPENING TIMES:
Sun & public holidays
Easter–end Oct: 2–5;
Nov–Easter: 2–4
(weather permitting)
FACILITIES: Museum
DISABLED: Phone in
advance

INSTOW SIGNAL BOX was built about 1873 to control the crossing gates and passing loop at Instow Station. It was replaced in 1979 by automatic signalling and, after years of neglect, the interior has been fully restored, with its levers, gate wheel and instruments, and is now managed and opened to the public by members of the Bideford & Instow Railway Group. The Box is Grade II listed, the first in the UK. Visitors can now "pull off" a reinstated signal. The lattice Signal Post has been restored to its original position across the road from the Signal Box and there are plans to reconnect this as soon as funds permit.

IRONBRIDGE GORGE MUSEUM

HOW TO FIND US:
By car: Off M54
Car parking: On site
By bus: Midland Red and Elcocks
ADDRESS:
Ironbridge, Telford, Shropshire TF8 7AW
TEL: 01952 433522
WEBSITE: www. ironbridge.org.uk/
OPENING TIMES:
Summer: 10–6 daily; winter: 10–5
FACILITIES:
Licensed Victorian pub, sweet shop and tea rooms
DISABLED:
Wheelchair access and adapted toilets

THE QUIET SHROPSHIRE town of Coalbrookdale became, in the late 18th century, the birthplace of the Industrial Revolution. The town, which would soon become the biggest iron-making centre in the world, produced the world's first iron rails, boats and trains and, indeed, the first iron bridge; an accomplishment which so impressed the local inhabitants that they renamed the town after it. The fabulous Ironbridge Museum is spread over a 50-acre, six-mile-long site at Blists Hill. The principal railway exhibit is a replica of the first ever steam rail locomotive (produced some 26 years before Stephenson's "Rocket"), designed by Richard Trevithick and built in Ironbridge in 1802.

ISLE OF WIGHT

HOW TO FIND US:
By car: Clearly signed
Car parking: Free at Havenstreet Station
By rail: Island Line to Smallbrook Junction
By bus: Southern Vectis Route 7; Westbrook Travel Route 88
By ferry: From Portsmouth (connects with Island Line trains at Ryde)
ADDRESS: Havenstreet, Isle of Wight, PO33 4DS
TEL: 01983 882204
FAX: 01983 884515
INFOLINE: 01983 884343
WEBSITE: www. iwsteamrailway.co.uk
LENGTH OF LINE: 5 miles
OPENING TIMES:
Jun–Sep: daily; Mar–May & Oct: selected days
FACILITIES: Licensed café, gift shop
DISABLED: Call ahead

PASSENGER TRAINS ON this railway are operated exclusively using beautifully restored Victorian and Edwardian carriages, usually hauled by Victorian locomotives, all of which have spent most of their working lives on the Island. Trains run from Smallbrook Junction (where it connects with Island Line's Ryde to Shanklin electric trains), through Ashey and Havenstreet to Wootton Station, a delightful country terminus complete with old wooden booking office and signal box. All facilities are at Havenstreet, where there is also a play area and woodland walk. The Railway hosts a number of special events throughout the year.

HOW TO FIND US:
By car: NE of
Bradford on A650
Car parking: Free
By rail: Leeds

ADDRESS: Haworth,
Keighley, West Yorks
BD22 8NJ

TEL: 01535 645214

INFOLINE: 01535 647777

WEBSITE: www.
kwvr.co.uk

LENGTH OF LINE:
4.75 miles

OPENING TIMES:
All year: w/ends &
public holidays;
mid Jun–early Sep: daily

FACILITIES: Shops,
buffets, picnic areas,
Pullman dining car
(advance booking
essential: reservations
on 01706 878512)

DISABLED:
Wheelchair access by
prior arrangement

Britain's last remaining complete branch line railway runs from Keighley to Oxenhope, along a rich seam of West Yorkshire's rail and cultural heritage. Travel via Ingrow, with its award-winning Museum of Rail Travel and workshops, and Damems, the country's smallest station, to Oakworth where *The Railway Children* was filmed, a superb example of an Edwardian Station, complete with authentic advertising signs, gas lighting and coal fires. From here, ride on to Haworth, home to another famous family – the Brontës. There is a station shop and you can catch bus service 812 which links the station to Pendon Mill, the Parsonage and the shops on summer Sundays and bank holidays. From September 2000, a major Heritage Lottery funded development at Oxenhope will place the reserve collection of rolling stock out of public access for 18 months. The line terminates at Oxenhope, where there is a buffet and picnic site. Why not take the Railway Children Walk which links Oakworth, Haworth and Oxenhope.

HOW TO FIND US:
By car: A28 between
Ashford & Hastings
Car parking: Free park-
ing available at
Tenterden and Northiam
By rail/bus: Ashford;
from here take no. 400
to Tenterden
ADDRESS:
Kent & East Sussex
Railway, Tenterden,
Kent TN30 6HE
TEL: 01580 765155
INFOLINE: 01580 762943
WEBSITE: www.
seetb.org.uk/kesr
LENGTH OF LINE:
10.5 miles
OPENING TIMES:
Mar: Sun;
Apr, May & Oct: w/ends
& public holidays;
Jun & Sep: Tue–Thu &
w/ends;
Jul & Aug: daily
FACILITIES: Café
DISABLED:
Disabled parking,
adapted toilets,
wheelchair access to
carriages

THE FIRST LINE to be built under the Light Railways Act of 1896 – and the first full size light railway in the world – the Kent and East Sussex Railway opened in 1900. It has been carefully restored by a team of dedicated volunteers, and now carries passengers in beautifully restored coaches dating from Victorian times to the 1960s. through more than 10 scenic miles of Kentish countryside from Tenterden, through Northiam to Bodiam (home of the National Trust's most picturesque castle). A "must-see" is the Colonel Stephens Railway Museum beside Tenterden Town Station, an exhibition detailing the life and work of the enigmatic founder of this and many other great railways. This award-winning museum also houses the "Gazelle" – the smallest standard gauge steam engine in the world. There are many steam links with other local attractions such as the vineyards at Biddenden and the South of England Rare Breeds Centre at Woodchurch.

KEW BRIDGE STEAM MUSEUM

HOW TO FIND US:
Underground:
Gunnersbury or Kew
Bridge
By rail: Kew Bridge
By bus: Nos 65, 237
267, 391
ADDRESS:
Green Dragon Lane,
Brentford,
Middlesex TW8 0EN
TEL: 020 8568 4757
WEBSITE: www.
kbsm.org.uk
LENGTH OF LINE: 100 yds
OPENING TIMES:
11–5 daily; call for
information
FACILITIES:
Café at weekends
DISABLED: Limited
wheelchair access,
large print guide for the
visually impaired

THIS UNIQUE MUSEUM focuses on the development of London's water supply from Roman times to the Thames Ring Main. It houses a wonderful collection of Victorian water-pumping machinery, including magnificent Cornish beam engines, and the Water for Life Gallery in which you can view replicas of the London sewer system. Many Victorian waterworks had their own steam railways and locomotives and examples of these are displayed on a short stretch of line featuring "Cloister", a Hunslet engine, and "Wendy", a Bagnall engine.

KIRKLEES

HOW TO FIND US:
By car: Clayton West is
on the A636 Wakefield/
Denby Dale Road
Car parking: Free
By rail: Denby Dale.
By bus: 235 from
Huddersfield and 484
from Wakefield
ADDRESS: Kirklees Light
Railway Company Co.
Ltd, Clayton West,
nr Huddersfield, West
Yorkshire HD8 9XJ
TEL: 01484 865727
LENGTH OF LINE: 4 miles
OPENING TIMES:
All year: w/ends;
Spring public holiday–
early Sep and most
school holidays: daily
FACILITIES:
Café and souvenir shop
DISABLED: Limited
wheelchair access

THIS PURPOSE BUILT 15" gauge railway has been laid on the old Lancashire & York-shire Clayton West branch line which used to feed the main Huddersfield–Sheffield line. From Clayton West, half-size steam trains run through four miles of gently rolling countryside, passing through a 500-yd tunnel on the way. There is a network of country walks in the surrounding area and picnic facilities are provided at both ends. A visitor centre opened in 1998, where the history of the line and area are explained. There is also an ornamental pond encircled by a model railway.

LAKESIDE & HAVERTHWAITE

HOW TO FIND US:
By car: Junction 36 off the M6 and
follow the signs on the A590 Newby Bridge Road
Car parking: £1 per day
By rail: Ulverston

ADDRESS:
Haverthwaite
Station, NrUlverston,
Cumbria LA12 8AL

TEL: 01539 531594

LENGTH OF LINE:
3.5 miles

OPENING TIMES:
Easter school holidays
and May–Oct: daily;
specials in Dec

FACILITIES: Souvenir
shop, picnic area,
refreshments

ARGUABLY THE COUNTRY'S most scenic journey, from the Victorian station at Haverthwaite hard-working steam locomotives haul comfortable coaches through the ever chaning lake and river scenery of the beautiful Leven valley. A varied seletion of steam and diesel loomotives are on display at Haverthwaite station. From the terminus at Lakeside there is an opportunity to continue your trip aboard one of the Windermere Lake Cruises elegant 1930s steamers for a tour around England's largest and most beautiful lake. There is a variety of attractions bordering the lake including the Windermere Steamboat Museum, the Lake District National Park Visitor Centre, with its 30 acres of terraced gardens, and the Aquarium of the lakes, home to the largest collection of freshwater fish in England.

LAPPA VALLEY

HOW TO FIND US:
By car: Signposted
from A3075 Newquay to
Redruth Road and from
A30 and A3058
Car parking: Free
By bus: Newquay (late
May–late Sep, Mon–Fri)
ADDRESS: Lappa Valley
Steam Railway, St New-
lyn East, Newquay,
Cornwall TR8 5HZ
TEL: 01872 51031
WEBSITE: www.
lappa-railway.co.uk
LENGTH OF LINE:
15" gauge: 1 mile
10.25" gauge: 748 yds
7.25" gauge: 350 yds
OPENING TIMES:
Mid Apr–end Oct: daily
FACILITIES: Gift shop,
licensed coffee shop,
9-hole golf course
DISABLED: Call ahead

THE LAPPA VALLEY Steam Railway lies in a tranquil rural valley, running on one of the oldest trackbeds in Cornwall, opened in 1849 as a mineral line from East Wheal Rose, a former silver lead mine, to Newquay. Today, beginning at Benny Halt, near St Newlyn East, catch one of two 15" gauge steam trains for a ride up the winding valley to the leisure park at East Wheal Rose. Here the visitor will find two other miniature train rides, as well as boating, crazy golf, a play area, brick path maze, picnic areas and country walks. A dramatic video provides an insight into the history of the mine.

LAUNCESTON

HOW TO FIND US:
By car: Off the A30
Car parking: At the
nearby Newport
Industrial Estate
By rail: Gunnislake
By bus: Sundays by
Nos 187 and 188
ADDRESS: Launceston
Steam Railway,
The Old Gasworks,
St Thomas's Road,
Launceston PL15 8DA
TEL: 01566 775665
LENGTH OF LINE:
2.5 miles
OPENING TIMES:
Easter–Whitsun & Oct:
Tue & Sun ;
Whitsun–end Sep: daily;
specials in Dec
FACILITIES: Buffet, gift
and book shop
DISABLED:
Wheelchair access to
most areas

THE FOUR LOCOMOTIVES maintained and run on this famous narrow gauge railway were built in the 1880s and '90s by the Hunslet Engine Company of Leeds, and worked carrying slate from the mountain quarries of North Wales. Nowadays they carry passengers from the winding hillside streets of Launceston through the glorious Cornish countryside – in open carriages on sunny days. The daily ticket allows plenty of opportunity for a meander along the local pathways or a quiet riverside picnic. There's plenty to do at Launceston, with workshops and a museum at the station, and walks over the river to the ancient priory.

LAVENDER LINE

HOW TO FIND US:
By car: Just off the A26
Car parking: On site
By rail: Lewes and
Uckfield
By bus: Buses from
Lewes and Uckfield
stop at the railway (no
service on Sun)
ADDRESS: Isfield Station,
Isfield, East Sussex
TN22 5XB
TEL: 01825 750515
LENGTH OF LINE: 1 mile
OPENING TIMES:
All year: Sun & public
holidays; Jul: Sat;
Aug: Wed, Thu, & Sat;
Santa trains in Dec
FACILITIES: Souvenir
shop, café, picnic area
disabled: Full wheel-
chair access.to site (no
disabled toilets)

Named not, as you might expect, because the trains wend their way through scented fields of purple flowers, but after the coal merchants who served the line – A.E. Lavender & Sons. The line was once part of the former Lewes–Uckfield Railway, which ran from 1858 to 1969. One mile of track has been relaid and the station restored to look as it would have done in the 1920s and '30s. There is a signal box, viewing area and a small museum housing various bits of railway paraphernalia in an 1860 Goods Office – the only such office in the country to have been restored and opened to the public.

LEEDS INDUSTRIAL MUSEUM

HOW TO FIND US:
By car: The Armley Mills
site is a few miles west
of Leeds, just off the
A651. It is signposted
Car parking: Adjacent to
the museum.
By rail: The nearest main
line station is Leeds, a
short bus ride away
By bus: Call Metro
0113 245 7676
ADDRESS:
Armley Mills, Canal
Road, Leeds LS12 2QF
TEL: 0113 263 7861
OPENING TIMES:
10–5 Tue-Sat; 1–5 Sun
FACILITIES: Museum
shop, refreshments,
picnic area
DISABLED: Wheelchair
access to most areas;
accessible toilets.
Guidedogs welcome.
Parking available

The Leeds Industrial Museum is housed in what was formerly the largest woollen mill in the world. From its spectacular river-side setting, the museum tells the story of the City's rich industrial past. The interior is dominated by the clanking and whirring of vast, restored textile industry machines, whilst outside there are regular demonstra-tions of static engines and steam locomo-tives. The museum also boasts displays cov-ering the Leeds' printing industry, replica workers' cottages and a fully restored 1920s' cinema. Vehicle sheds feature restored industrial locomotives and engines.

LEIGHTON BUZZARD

HOW TO FIND US:
By car: A4146
Car parking: Free
By rail: Leighton
Buzzard
By bus: Call for details
01234 228337
ADDRESS:
Billington Road,
Leighton Buzzard,
Beds LU7 8TN
TEL: 01525 373888
WEBSITE: www.
buzzrail.co.uk
LENGTH OF LINE: 3 miles
OPENING TIMES:
Sun and bank holidays
mid Mar–end Oct; Wed
in Jul, Tue–Thu in Aug
FACILITIES: Buffet, shop
DISABLED: Wheelchair
access to trains and
toilets

Deepest Bedfordshire, and the largest collection of narrow gauge locomotives in the country is put through its paces along the tight curves, steep gradients and level crossings of a country-roadside track. Here you can experience the English light railway as it was 80 years ago, with a wide variety of coaches and wagons in use and on display. There are many special events throughout the year, including a Teddy Bears' outing, a Steam Glow night, a photography event and the September Steam-Up.

LIGHTWATER VALLEY

HOW TO FIND US:
By car: A6108
Car parking: Free
By rail: Thirsk
ADDRESS:
North Stainley, Ripon,
N. Yorkshire HG4 3HT
TEL: 01765 635368
WEBSITE: www.
lightwatervalley.co.uk
OPENING TIMES:
Apr, May & Oct: w/ends;
Jun–Aug & school
holidays: daily
FACILITIES: Shopping
centre, various fast
food restaurants
DISABLED:
Wheelchair access to
park; adapted toilets

This jolly miniature steam railway, which gently winds its way through Lightwater Valley Theme Park, provides welcome relief from the surrounding adrenaline-soaked attractions. The park contains some truly terrifying rides, including "The Ultimate", the longest rollercoaster in the world; the coiled looping "Viper"; and "Sewer Rat", a subterranean rollercoaster. If the railway doesn't calm you down, you can always take a walk through some of the surrounding 175 acres of Yorkshire Dale woodland, or pay a visit to nearby Norton Conyers, a huge imposing medieval house that Charlotte Brontë used as the basis for Thornfield Hall in *Jane Eyre*.

LINCOLNSHIRE WOLDS

THIS IS A STANDARD gauge steam railway running on part of the orginal Great Northern Railway Grimsby to Louth line. It has two Peckett Industrial saddle tanks which provide passenger rides. Work is ongoing to extend to North Thoresby, a further mile away. The signal box and ticket office/museum have been rebuilt as near as possible to the original design. Rolling stock of varying ages can be seen, some in the process of being restored to their former glory in the Engine Shed. Many themed open days are held throughout the year.

MANGAPPS FARM RAILWAY MUSEUM

THIS FAMILY-RUN museum, on a working farm, summons up the past spirit of East Anglian railways. The historic buildings, moved from various sites in East Anglia and lovingly restored, include a complete working station and signal box. The museum itself contains one of the largest and most varied collections of railway memorabilia in the country, with signs, notices, posters, nameplates and signalling equipment, and a fascinating collection of relics from the Great Eastern Railway. There are locomotives and wagons ranging from the 1870s to the 1960s. A round trip is also available on the museum's preserved length of track.

MARKEATON PARK

HOW TO FIND US:
By car: Off A38, A52
Car parking: On site
By rail: Derby Station
By bus: R50, R51
ADDRESS: Markeaton
Park Light Railway,
Queensway, off A38,
Derby
TEL: 01623 552292
WEBSITE: www.
freespace.virgin.net/
david.lowe1/
markeatonpk.htm
LENGTH OF LINE:
Nearly 1 mile
OPENING TIMES:
Every weekend all year;
Derbyshire school
holidays
FACILITIES: Refresh-
ments, craft village,
playground, gardens
DISABLED:
Wheelchair access

THIS IS A GENUINE 15" narrow gauge steam railway which links Markeaton Park with the Mundy Play Centre. The journey between the two stations passes through tree-lined avenues and over the lake and stream bridges, giving excellent views of the lake, surrounding parkland and the local wildlife. Diesel trains may run on occasion. With canoes, rowing boats, crazy golf, a paddling pool (open Easter–Sep) and even donkeys, there is something for everyone in the family. Derby has a fine cathedral and, nearby, there are several National Trust properties to visit.

MIDDLETON

HOW TO FIND US:
By car: Immediately
adjacent to Jct 5 of
M621
Car parking: Free car
park at Moor Road
By rail: Leeds
By bus: Buses run to
the station from the
Leeds Corn Exchange
ADDRESS:
Middleton Railway,
Trust Ltd, Moor Road,
Leeds LS10 2JQ
TEL: 0113 2710320
LENGTH OF LINE:
1.25 miles
OPENING TIMES:
Apr–Oct: Sat, Sun &
public holidays
FACILITIES:
Souvenir shop
DISABLED:
Wheelchair access

THE MIDDLETON RAILWAY holds a number of records: built in 1758, it is the oldest working railway in the world and the first to be licensed by Parliament. In 1812 it became the first commercially successful steam railway; and, in 1960, having closed and fallen into disrepair, it was the first standard gauge railway to be reopened by volunteers. Today, visitors can take a trip of over a mile from Moor Road to Middleton Park Halt, where there is a picnic site, a nature trail and a children's playground. Special events are held throughout the year, including a "Day Out with Thomas", Easter Bunnies Weekend, Postman Pat's Special and Teddy Bears' Picnic.

HOW TO FIND US:
By car: Off the A31
Car parking: Car parking at Alresford and Alton Stations
By rail: Alton
By bus: Call
0345 023067

ADDRESS:
Mid-Hants Railway plc,
Railway Station,
Alresford,
Hants SO24 9JG

TEL: 01962 733810

INFOLINE: 01962 734866

WEBSITE: www.itoeye.co.uk

LENGTH OF LINE:
10 miles

OPENING TIMES:
Feb: Sun; Mar–Jun & Sep–Oct: w/ends & public holidays;
Jul & Aug: daily

FACILITIES: Café, book and souvenir shops, dining trains, licensed buffets on all main line trains

DISABLED: Wheelchair access at Alresford; adapted toilets

THIS RAILWAY IS also known as the "Watercress Line" because of the watercress beds which still grow in Alresford, a picturesque Georgian town and the railway's headquarters. You can travel from Winchester to Alresford by classic 1950s' bus on Saturdays from the beginning of June. The journey to Alton is about 10 miles, with two stops on the way. The first, Ropley, the engineering centre of the railway, is famous for its topiary and the site overlooking the station area is a prime spot for photographing the trains or having a picnic. At Medstead & Four Marks, at 630ft the highest station in Southern England, you can experience the steep climbs that the crews of yore called going 'Over the Alps'. From Alton, the Mid-Hants Railway links up with the national railway system and South West trains, running their own main line steam rail tours to such centres at the West Somerset Railway (Minehead), Brighton and Bristol.

MIDLAND RAILWAY CENTRE

HOW TO FIND US:
By car: 1 mile north of
Ripley on B6179
Car parking: At
Butterley Station
By rail: Derby or
Alfreton,
By bus: Trent services
91 or 92 from Derby,
91, 92, 93 and 94 from
Alfreton

ADDRESS:
Midland Railway Centre
Butterley Station,
Ripley,
Derbyshire DE5 3TL
TEL: 01773 570140
FAX: 01773 570721
INFOLINE: 01773 570140

LENGTH OF LINE:
Standard gauge:
3.5 miles;
2ft gauge: 1 mile

OPENING TIMES:
Static display all year:
10–4 daily; trains
operate all year:
w/ends & public
holidays; Apr–Oct: Wed;
school holidays: daily

FACILITIES:
Café, souvenir shops

DISABLED:
Wheelchair access to
station and coaches;
adapted toilets

THE MIDLAND RAILWAY CENTRE is very
different to most heritage railways. It
has a fine standard gauge railway which
runs from Butterley, through Swanwick
junction, along Golden Valley, terminating at Ironside, with magnificently
restored locomotives and rolling stock,
and it also boasts a huge
57-acre museum site. The museum site at
Swanwick Junction Station is accessed
either on foot from Butterley Station or
by alighting from one of the train rides. In
its exhibition hall is a collection of locomotives and rolling stock covering the
history of rail travel from the 1860s
onwards. There is also the Butterley Park
miniature railway and the Golden Valley
Light Railway, a narrow gauge line which
takes visitors through the 36-acre Country Park. Other exhibits include a large
model railway layout, a demonstration
signal box and a restored Victorian rail-
waymen's church.

HOW TO FIND US:
By car: Close to centre
of Dereham.
Car parking: Free
By rail: Norwich or
Wymondham
By bus: Contact Norfolk
Bus, 0845 300 6116

ADDRESS:
Railway Station, Station
Road, Dereham,
Norfolk, NR19 1DF
TEL: 01362 690633
LENGTH OF LINE:
11 miles
OPENING TIMES:
Sun all year, other days
in summer
FACILITIES:
Refreshments, souvenir
shop and museum
DISABLED:
Wheelchair access

A RELATIVE NEWCOMER TO the preserved railway scene, the Mid-Norfolk Railway is over 150 years old, and was part of the Great Eastern Railway network. The aim is to create a multi-functional railway serving tourists, freight customers and local passengers. This 11-mile branch line is now open between Dereham (the Railway's headquarters) and its junction with the main line at Wymondham, linking numerous villages and passing through four river valleys. The Trust hopes to run a passenger steam service from Dereham to Wymondham in the summer months.

MOORS VALLEY

HOW TO FIND US:
By car: The railway is
on the A31 via
Southampton, 3 miles
from the ring road
Car parking: On site
By rail: Bournemouth
By bus: X2

ADDRESS: Moors Valley
Country Park, Horton
Road, Ashley Heath,
Ringwood BH21 2ET
TEL: 01425 471415
LENGTH OF LINE: 1 mile
OPENING TIMES:
Mar–Oct: w/ends;
school holidays: daily;
Nov–Feb: Sun
FACILITIES: Buffet, model
shop at Kingsmere
DISABLED:
Wheelchair access to
site but not trains

I N THE SCENIC Moors Valley Park, this is the longest fully signalled narrow (7.25") gauge railway in the south of England. The ride takes you past, through and under sharp slopes, tunnels, level crossings, footbridges and signal boxes. There are two stations, Lakeside and Kingsmere, the latter boasting a goods yard, engine shed and workshop. There is also a model shop supplying such names as Hornby, Bachmann and Peco. The park itself features an adventure playground, lakeside picnic areas, 18-hole golf course and forest walks.

MUSEUM OF ARMY TRANSPORT

HOW TO FIND US:
By car: Just off the
A164 Hull–Beverley
Road;
Car parking: On site
By rail: Beverley
ADDRESS: Museum of
Army Transport,
Flemingate, Beverley,
East Yorkshire
HU17 0NG
TEL: 01482 860445
OPENING TIMES:
10–5 daily
FACILITIES: Cafeteria,
souvenir shop
DISABLED: Wheelchair
access to the floor of
the museum, if not all
the exhibits; adapted
toilets

A HUGE TWO-ACRE hangar full of planes, tanks, jeeps, cars and, of course, trains displayed in various mock-combat settings. You are allowed to clamber inside many of the vehicles, including the museum's largest exhibit, the Blackburn Beverley aircraft. Other items of interest include Montgomery's Rolls-Royce, an SAS Pink Panther and an army transport narrow gauge railway; the museum also holds a fascinating archive of army railway memorabilia. Children will enjoy the model exhibition – over 6,000 beautifully crafted miniature fighting machines

MUSEUM OF SCIENCE & INDUSTRY

HOW TO FIND US:
By car: The museum is
in Castlefield, close to
Manchester city centre
Car parking: On site
By rail: Deansgate
ADDRESS:
Museum of Science &
Industry in Manchester,
Liverpool Road,
Castlefield,
Manchester M3 4FP
TEL: 0161 8322244
INFOLINE: 0161 8321830
WEBSITE: www.
msim.org.uk
OPENING TIMES:
10–5 daily; steam rides
may not be running due
to renovation work
FACILITIES:
Restaurant, museum
shop, picnic areas
DISABLED: 95% wheelchair access, adapted
toilets

THE MUSEUM OF Science & Industry in Manchester is housed in the world's oldest passenger railway station. This enormous museum is crammed full of whirring, buzzing gizmos and gadgets designed to tell the

story of one of the world's great industrial cities. There's a four-storey electricity gallery, a fabric and fashion gallery, an "Air and Space Hall" with a reconstructed biplane and a flight simulator, an interactive science gallery – guaranteed to keep children enthralled for hours – and, in the basement, a reconstructed Victorian sewer complete with authentic sounds and smells. On Sundays there are rides on some of the Museum's original and replica steam engines, including a version of George Stephenson's "Planet" – the locomotive that caused the world's first passenger rail death when it backed over Liverpool MP William Huskisson just before its maiden journey.

NATIONAL RAILWAY MUSEUM

HOW TO FIND US:
By car: signed from
York's ring road
Car parking: On site
By rail: York
By bus: From York
Minster Apr–Oct

ADDRESS:
Leeman Road,
York YO26 4XJ

TEL: 01904 621261

WEBSITE:
www.nmsi.ac.uk/nrm

OPENING TIMES:
10–6 daily

FACILITIES: Gift shop,
restaurant, café

DISABLED: Wheelchair
access to most parts of
the museum, wheelchair
loan available

ONE OF THE MAIN problems with the National Railway Museum is that there is so much to see and do. It is not alone in this respect, but, unless you keep your eyes and ears open and your wits about you, there is little doubt that you will need to pay a return visit. In fact, even if you do manage to view most exhibits, it is a mistake to think that one visit is sufficient; the continually changing displays mean that there is always something new to see.

Whichever entrance you use (there are two), the initial question is where would be best to go first? If there is something specific that you wish to see, use one of the two Information Points indicated on your entry ticket or ask one of the guides (staff normally in red tops) for directions. Otherwise, you would be well advised to find one of the many strategically placed old railway seats to study the museum plan and just look around at the sheer scale of the place. Many of the seats are located in front of video

screens and most of the programmes shown last between five and ten minutes; watching one of these will help set the mood for what is to come. Later in your visit, watching others will prove extremely beneficial to tired limbs.

The museum is split into three main sections, the Great Hall, the Station Hall and the Works, but there is a certain amount of overlap in the types of exhibits to be found in each. For instance, the Great Hall is the main display area for locomotives (there are at least 20 different types to be seen around the turntable alone), but other examples are to be found in both the Station Hall and in the Works, where they are displayed to illustrate the theme of those particular locations.

Each section is divided into subsections, each with a fascinating story to tell; once again there are overlaps, but these are inevitable in order to explain the complex and interwoven development of the railways.

For most of the course of its development over the greater part of the last two centuries, the railway industry has had to be all things to all men. In simple terms, it has carried the

population to work and to leisure; and it has transported raw materials of all kinds to factories and production units and finished products to the consumer. In order to live up to these expectations, the industry has been required to develop, and invest in, all manner of new thinking and new technology, a process which goes on to this day.

The museum displays make a first-class effort at condensing all the chapters of this fascinating history into what is, despite first impressions, a relatively small area. There are reminders of a wide variety of equipment and practices which evoke nostaliga from the grandparents and disbelieving looks from the grandchildren. But it this is an ongoing story; not only will you find a reconstruction of the earliest, medieval wooden railways with their human motive power, but also a section of the Channel Tunnel and the front end of a Eurostar train. There is an early Royal Coach dating from the 1840s together with one from the 1940s which was used by HM The Queen as late as 1977. There are illustrations of the earliest forms of primitive signalling in use at the dawn of the Railway Age while, adjacent to the trackside balcony in the Works, there is a direct link to the present Signalling Centre, which controls all trains in the York Area.

And then there are the models! Even if your interest lies in the evolution of the full

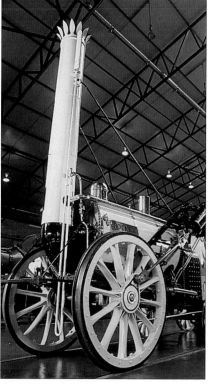

sized railway you cannot fail to be impressed by the sheer numbers of scale models which abound. Some, built to extremely fine exhibition standard, demonstrate specialist engineering workshop skills and were used to promote the achievements and professionalism of the early private railway companies; others are used to illustrate particular showcase themes or as examples of the expertise of the dedicated amateur enthusiast.

A fine array of railway clocks, strategically located, and all in perfect working order, demonstrate how much you are enjoying yourself by providing frequent reminders of how quickly your visit is passing.

Aladdin had his cave of treasures; we have the National Railway Museum. Unfortunately you will not be able to rub a magic lamp and be transported to the door, but, whatever effort is required to get there, your endeavour will be more than adequately rewarded. It is, after all, the best railway museum in the world.

NENE VALLEY

HOW TO FIND US:

By car: Just off the A1 between the A47 and A605 junctions

Car parking: On-site

By rail: Peterborough

ADDRESS:

Wansford Station, Stibbington, Peterborough PE8 6LR

TEL: 01780 784444

INFOLINE: 01780 784440

LENGTH OF LINE:

7.5 miles

OPENING TIMES:

End Feb–Mar: w/ends;
Apr–Oct: Wed & w/ends;
Jul–Aug: Tue–Sun

FACILITIES: Café, museum shop, second hand bookshop

DISABLED: Wheelchair access to all facilities and trains

THE NENE VALLEY RAILWAY is one of the country's most famous railways and has been the location for dozens of films and TV programmes, including *Octopussy*, *Goldeneye* and *London's Burning*. It is also the home of "Thomas", perhaps the best loved of all train engines, who has his own special events through the year. Visitors can take a ride starting at Wansford, with its engine shed, unique collection of historic European locomotives, and model railway. The trains pass through scenic Yarwell, on to Ferry Meadows (the new station) which gives access to the Country Park with acres of meadows, lakes, woods, activity areas and a miniature railway, and then on board again to Orton Mere, with its model boating lake and canoe slalom course. The more energetic visitor will find a pleasant one-mile, tree-lined walk from Ferry Meadows to Orton Mere, where a further short stroll will take you to Thorpe Meadows. The final leg of the journey takes passengers to the end of the line at the beautifully restored Peterborough NVR station.

NATIONAL TRAMWAY MUSEUM

HOW TO FIND US:
By car: Crich is 8 miles from the M1 near Matlock.
Car parking: On site
By rail: Cromford
By bus: local bus: call Busline 01332 292200
ADDRESS:
Crich, Matlock, Derbyshire DE4 5DP
TEL: 01773 852565
LENGTH OF LINE: 1 mile
OPENING TIMES:
Apr–Oct: 10–5.30
Mon–Fri; 10–6.30 Sat, Sun & public holidays
FACILITIES: Souvenir shop, bookshop, picnic areas
DISABLED: A special access tram has been fitted out to carry people with mobility difficulties

S ET IN THE delightful village of Crich in the heart of the Derbyshire countryside, the National Tramway Museum is the proud owner of the largest collection of preserved trams in Europe—over 70 horse-drawn, steam and electric models gathered from all over the world. When you arrive you are given a vintage penny which you use to pay for your first ride along a one-mile length of track passing through a recreated tram-era street, under the elegant Bowes-Lyon bridge and then out into some wonderful open countryside. Part of the tram line occupies the route of a narrow gauge mineral railway built by George Stephenson. More trams can be found in the large exhibition hall where there is also an interactive display on the history of the tram.

NORTH WOOLWICH

HOW TO FIND US:
By car: No parking, so travel by alternative means
By rail: North Woolwich
By bus: 101, 473
By boat: Woolwich Free Ferry
ADDRESS: Pier Road, North Woolwich, London E16 2JJ
TEL: 020 7474 7244
FAX: 020 7473 6065
OPENING TIMES:
Jan–Nov: 1–5 w/ends; school holidays:1–5 Mon–Wed (closed winter school holidays)
FACILITIES: Shop
DISABLED: Wheelchair access and adapted toilets

T HE NORTH WOOL-WICH Old Station Museum offers a revealing glimpse into the golden age of London's railway. It is housed in a very large, very grand Italianate rail terminus, first built in 1847 and restored to its former glory in the 1970s and 1980s. There are two platforms, a waiting room, a ladies' waiting room and a ticket office, all beautifully recreated with much of the original furniture still in place. Various artifacts relating to the history of rail are on display in replica wooden ticket offices. Outside are several locomotives and carriages from the late 19th and early 20th centuries including a Royal Arsenal Ammunition Wagon.

NORTH NORFOLK

HOW TO FIND US:
By car: A148 Cromer to
Holt road and follow the
brown tourist signs
Car parking: On site
By rail: Sheringham

ADDRESS:
Sheringham, Norfolk
NR26 8RA

TEL: 01263 822045

INFOLINE: 01263 825449

WEBSITE: www.
nnrailway.co.uk

LENGTH OF LINE:
5.25 miles

OPENING TIMES:
Mar: w/ends;
Apr–Oct: daily Nov: Sat;;
Santa and mince pie
Specials in Dec

FACILITIES:
Buffet at Weybourne;
bookshop, souvenir
shop, railway model
shop at Sheringham
Disabled: Wheelchair
access, including trains

THE NORTH NORFOLK RAILWAY, or "Poppy Line" as it is affectionately known, is a full-size steam railway running along the beautiful Norfolk coast from Sheringham, where there is a small steam railway museum and demonstration signal box, to the charming Georgian town of Holt. At Holt, visitors can watch the engine run round the coaches. You can either walk into Holt, catch a horse drawn bus or a bus from the nearby bus stop. On the way, you can stop off at Weybourne Station, a perfect picnic spot in the middle of some delightful woodland countryside. The Railway also offers trips aboard two sumptuous 1940s Brighton Belle Pullman restaurant cars which run between Sheringham and Holt on most Saturday nights and Sunday lunchtimes during the season. The railway holds special days when you can learn how to drive a steam engine or diesel loco, or operate a signal box.

HOW TO FIND US:
By car: Pickering
Station is on the A170
between Scarborough
and Thirsk
Car parking: At car
parks at Pickering,
Levisham, Goathland
and Grosmont
By rail: Grosmont
ADDRESS:
Pickering Station,
Pickering,
North Yorkshire
YO18 7AJ
TEL: 01751 472508
WEBSITE: www.
nymr.demon.co.uk
LENGTH OF LINE:
18 miles
OPENING TIMES:
Daily late Mar–Oct
FACILITIES: Shops and
refreshments at
Pickering, Goathland
and Grosmont
DISABLED:
Wheelchair access

THIS WAS FORMERLY part of the Midland and Great Northern Joint Railway. It runs through the beautiful North Yorkshire Moors National Park from Pickering, a lovely Yorkshire market town (the lively street market is held every Monday) set beneath a medieval castle, through Levisham, the gateway to Newton Dale and its stunning glacial valley, Goathland, the scenic rural village featured in TV's *Heartbeat*; and on to Grosmont, the operational headquarters where various locomotives, including the 1943 "Vera Lynn", can be viewed in the engine shed. There are various special events held throughout the year including a Thomas the Tank Engine weekend, a vintage car weekend and brass band concerts in the Levisham Station paddock. The Railway also provides a luxurious first class Pullman Dining service and you can even rent a camping coach at Goatland station which offers ideal accomodation for a family of four

NORTHAMPTON AND LAMPORT

HOW TO FIND US:
By car: 5 miles north of Northampton off A5159
Car parking: On site.
By rail/bus: Not served by public transport
ADDRESS: Pitsford & Brampton Station, Pitsford Road, Chapel Brampton, Northants NN6 8BA
TEL: 01604 820327
WEBSITE: www.nlr.org.uk
LENGTH OF LINE: 0.75 miles
OPENING TIMES: Steam and classic diesel service Mar–Dec: Sun & public holidays; special events and fun w/ends through the year
FACILITIES: Buffet, gift shop, refreshments
DISABLED: Call ahead

DESIGNED BY THE two great railway Georges, Bidder and Stephenson, and opened in 1859, the Northampton and Lamport Railway operated as a passenger line for over 120 years. In 1981 work began on its restoration and in 1996 it reopened to the public. Today it is home to a number of steam and diesel locomotives, the oldest built in 1933, which chug up and down a 0.75-mile section of track – work on an extension will begin soon. The Brampton Valley Way, a country footpath and cycleway, runs alongside allowing access to the surrounding countryside.

NORTHANTS IRONSTONE RAILWAY TRUST

HOW TO FIND US:
By car: Just off the M1, 3 miles south of Northampton
Car parking: On site
By rail: Northampton
By bus: nos 24, 25 & 26
ADDRESS:
West Hunsbury, Hunsbury Hill Road, Camp Hill, Northampton
TEL: 01604 702031
LENGTH OF LINE: 2.25 miles
OPENING TIMES:
Open throughout the year; train service Apr–Sep: Sun & public holidays; Santa Specials in Dec
FACILITIES: Café, shop, picnic area, children's play area
DISABLED: Coaches allow wheelchair access

HERE, IN A NORTHAMPTONSHIRE country park, the relics of the county's ironstone industry have been painstakingly preserved. The ironworks were in existence from 1873 until 1921 when first horses, and then steam-powered locomotives, pulled wagons full of iron ore along a two-mile quarryside track. The railway was restored in the 1970s and a passenger service started in 1982. The Trust is home to a Bulleid double-decker train, Kitson and Hunslett locos, several industrial shunting locomotives, a class 121 DTS, and a collection of Southern Region coaches. The museum also displays photographs and documents relating to the ironstone industry.

NOTTS TRANSPORT HERITAGE CENTRE

HOW TO FIND US:
By car: 3 miles south of Nottingham
Car parking: On site.
By rail/bus: Nottingham call 0115 924 0000

ADDRESS:
Mere Way, Ruddington, Nottingham, NG11 6NX
TEL: 0115 940 5705
WEBSITE: www. nthc.org.uk
LENGTH OF LINE: 3 miles
OPENING TIMES:
Mid-Apr–mid-Oc: 10.45–5 Sun & public holidayst
FACILITIES: Shop and café, picnic area, country park walks
DISABLED: Wheelchair access, toilets

THE ONLY STEAM railway in Nottinghamshire runs from the Heritage Centre through Rushcliffe Country Park and down the old Great Central Railway main line to Gotham Moor, a pleasant six-mile round trip. The purchase of a further five miles of track is nearing completion and will extend the journey to Rushcliffe Halt and eventually Loughborough (North). At the Heritage Centre, there is a collection of vintage and classic buses, as well as a superb triple gauge miniature railway. Surrounding it are a network of walks and a wildlife lake.

PEAK RAIL

HOW TO FIND US:
By car: M1, take Jct 28 to Matlock
Car parking: Matlock, Darley Dale and Rowsley South stations (200 spaces at latter)
By rail: Matlock
By bus: From Nottingham
ADDRESS: Matlock Station, Matlock, Derbyshire DE4 3NA
TEL: 01629 580381
LENGTH OF LINE: 4.5 miles
OPENING TIMES: All year; Sun: Apr–Oct: w/ends; Jun–Jul: Wed, w/ends; Aug: Tue–Thu, w/ends
FACILITIES: Cafés, shops, picnic area, children's play area, and riverside walks at Rowsley South
DISABLED: Wheelchair access on trains, toilets

UNTIL 1968, WHEN the express route from St Pancras to Manchester finished and the track was torn up, Midland Railway operated one of the best-loved steam routes in the country, through the heart of Derby-

shire's Peak District. Since 1978 Peak Rail has been working towards reopening the route from Matlock to Buxton, currently running on the scenic section between Matlock Riverside, Darley Dale and Rowsley (the focal point of Peak Rail's activities). Travel in the luxurious surroundings of a restored Palatine Restaurant coach or take a more hands-on approach in the earthier atmosphere of the locomotive engine itself.

62

HOW TO FIND US:
By car: M5, then follow
signs for Paignton
Car parking: Car park in
Paignton, and car parks
in Goodrington and
Kingswear
By rail: Paignton
ADDRESS:
Dart Valley Railway plc,
Queen's Park Station,
Paignton,
Devon TQ4 6AF
TEL: 01803 553760
LENGTH OF LINE: 7 miles
OPENING TIMES:
Easter–Oct, as well as
Santa Specials in Dec
FACILITIES:
Refreshment
facilities at Paignton
and Kingswear
DISABLED:
Wheelchair access

THE HOLIDAY LINE with a difference – steam trains and boats. This steam railway offers the discerning traveller many options. Take a steam train along the dramatic Torbay coastline from Paignton, travelling through Goodrington and Churston, and along the wooded slopes beside the Dart estuary to Kingswear from where you can take the ferry across to Dartmouth, a river cruise to Totnes and back by open-topped bus to Paignton. Whilst in historic Dartmouth, take a cruise around the harbour and view the Royal Naval College, Bayard's Cove and Dartmouth Castle. Travellers can choose to make the round trip, have a river cruise, or return to Paignton by steam train. There are many special events organised, and there is the luxury Riviera Belle dining train for that special occasion.

PERRYGROVE

HOW TO FIND US:
By car: South of Cole-
ford, Glos on the B4228
Car parking: On site
By rail: Lydney
By bus: Stagecoach
Red & White No. 31
(Gloucester to Coleford)
phone 01633 266336

ADDRESS:
Perrygrove Railway,
Coleford,
Glos GL16 8QB

TEL: 01594 834991

LENGTH OF LINE:
0.75 miles

OPENING TIMES: Most
Sun during the year
plus school holidays;
phone for timetable

FACILITIES: Café, indoor
children's area, all-
weather treasure hunt

DISABLED: Wheelchair
access on trains

THE PERRYGROVE RAILWAY is best described
as a cross between a miniature railway
and a full-blown steam railway – a sort of
"teenage" railway – and, as a result, is
hugely popular with children and adults
alike. Although the train runs on 15" gauge
track, the engine is still large enough to
allow the driver to stand upright, the only
locomotive of its kind where the driver can
do this. The track itself, laid out on the edge
of the Forest of Dean, runs through farm-
land and woods to the site of a disused iron
mine, and includes two sections with 1 in
30 gradients.

PLYM VALLEY

HOW TO FIND US:
By car: 5 miles from
Plymouth centre
Car parking: On-site
By rail: Plymouth
By bus: nos 20, 20A,
21, 22A and 51 run
from Plymouth

ADDRESS: Marsh Mills
Station, Coypool Road,
Marsh Mills, Plymouth,
Devon PL7 4NL

TEL: 01503 250539

WEBSITE: www.
plymrail.co.uk

LENGTH OF LINE:
0.5 miles

OPENING TIMES:
11 most Sun

FACILITIES:
Shop and refreshments
at Marsh Mills station

DISABLED:
Wheelchair access to
platform and trains

THE PLYM VALLEY RAILWAY is a reconstruction of part of the former Great Western Railway's Tavistock branch line (closed
to passenger traffic in 1962) which ran
through some delightful leafy Devon countryside. So far, a new station, locomotive
shed and sidings have been built and half a
mile of track relaid. The aim is to reopen
the 1.5 miles of track from Marsh Mills to
Plym Bridge, and it is hoped a service will
begin operating during 2001, using a wide
variety of steam and diesel locomotives
including Falmouth Docks No.3 – the last
steam locomotive to be in industrial use in
southwest England.

RAVENGLASS AND ESKDALE

HOW TO FIND US:
By car: A595 West
Cumbrian coast road
between Barrow-in-
Furness and Whitehaven
Car parking: On site
By rail: Ravenglass.
ADDRESS: Ravenglass
and Eskdale Railway,
Ravenglass,
Cumbria CA18 1SW
TEL: 01229 717171
WEBSITE: www.
ravenglkass-railway.co.uk
LENGTH OF LINE: 7 miles
OPENING TIMES: Mid-
Mar–Oct: daily; Nov–mid-
Mar: phone for details
FACILITIES: Pub, railway
museum at Ravenglass;
souvenir shop and café
in Eskdale
DISABLED: Wheelchair
access to some coach-
es; adapted toilets

ORIGINALLY BUILT TO carry iron ore from mines in Eskdale, the Ravenglass and Eskdale Railway, known locally as "La'al Ratty", is today one of the most popular tourist lines in the country. The journey begins at Ravenglass, home to a first-century Roman bath house, passing through Muncaster with its medieval castle and 15th-century working water-mill, and then out into the rich Cumbrian countryside of rugged mountains, dry stone walls, crystal-clear rivers and waterfalls, before coming to rest at Eskdale, site of the famous Hardknott Fort, built by the Romans in *c*100 BC.

ROYAL VICTORIA

HOW TO FIND US:
By car: Brown tourist
signs from Jct 8 off
M27 or A27
Car parking: Four pay &
display car parks in the
Royal Victoria Country
Park
By rail: Netley
ADDRESS: Royal
Victoria Country Park,
Netley SO31 5GA
TEL: 02380 456246
LENGTH OF LINE: 1 mile
OPENING TIMES:
All year: w/ends &
school holidays from
11.30 onwards
FACILITIES: Tea rooms
and picnic areas in the
park
DISABLED:
Wheelchair access; a
special leaflet for the
disabled is available on
request

THIS SPRIGHTLY AND colourful miniature railway was built in 1995 and operates around a one-mile circuit in the Royal Victoria Country Park – there are plans for a further half-mile extension. It is aimed principally at children – the line circles a children's play area and all the engines have cute names such as Maurice the Major and Claud the Colonel – but adults will be able to appreciate the glorious country park setting overlooking Southampton Water. Nearby, in the country park, a 100-ft tower offers some stupendous panoramic views of the Hampshire countryside and out over the sea to the Isle of Wight.

HOW TO FIND US:
By car: Hythe Station is
3 miles from the M20,
Jct 11.
Car parking: On site
By rail/bus:
Folkestone Central,
then bus to Hythe
ADDRESS:
New Romney Station,
Kent TN28 8PL
TEL: 01797 362353
WEBSITE: www.
rhdr.demon.co.uk
LENGTH OF LINE:
13.5 miles
OPENING TIMES:
W/ends in Feb; daily
Mar-Oct; Santa specials
in Dec
FACILITIES: Cafés and
souvenir shops
DISABLED: Wheelchair
access on trains, but
call in advance;
adapted toilets

THE ROMNEY, HYTHE AND DYMCHURCH Railway is a true historical oddity; a miniature railway, built in the 1920s for the racing car driver Captain Howey. It opened in 1927 as "The World's Smallest Public Railway", a triumph of miniature engineering with one-third size locomotives hauling coaches at high speeds across historic Romney March. Captain Howey had hoped to operate it as a full mainline railway carrying freight as well as passengers. Unfortunately, British industry did not share his vision and the railway was forced to rely on holiday-makers for its main source of income. It was used by the army during World War II, and reopened in 1946. Today, it can claim the honour of being the world's longest 15" gauge railway, running across Romney Marsh from Hythe to Dungeness, passing through New Romney, with its famous Toy and Model Museum, on the way.

RUISLIP LIDO

HOW TO FIND US:
By car: Follow signs for
A4180 (B469) from A40
Car parking: Available
approximately 50yds
from Ruislip Lido
(Water's Edge) Station
By Underground: Metro-
politan and Piccadilly
Lines from London and
Uxbridge.
By bus: H13 from Ruislip
ADDRESS:
Ruislip Lido Railway,
Reservoir Road, Ruislip,
Middx HA4 7TY
TEL: 020 8866 9654
INFOLINE: 01895 622595
LENGTH OF LINE: 2 miles
OPENING TIMES:
Year round service
FACILITIES: Family pub,
picnic areas, shop
DISABLED: Wheelchair
access to trains

THE RUISLIP LIDO RAILWAY is a volunteer-run 12" narrow gauge line. It runs from Ruislip Lido Station, near the car park, to Woody Bay Station by the beach. It is hard to believe that all the bustle of London is nearby as the journey takes you through pleasant woodland and around the far end of the lake to the re-creational area on the beach side. The operational steam locomotive is based on the Hunslet "Blanche" as used on the Ffestiniog Railway.

RUTLAND RAILWAY MUSEUM

HOW TO FIND US:
By car: 4 miles north of
Oakham between Ash-
well and Cottesmore
Car parking: On site
By rail: Oakham
ADDRESS:
Ashwell Road,
Cottesmore, Oakham,
Rutland LE15 7BX
TEL: 01572 813203
LENGTH OF LINE:
0.75 miles
OPENING TIMES:
All year: 11–5 w/ends;
phone for details of
steam days
FACILITIES:
Refreshments,
picnic sites, shop
DISABLED: No facilities

IN THE LATE 19th century and for much of the 20th, ironstone mining was one of Rutland's principal industries and the Museum site was the loading point for ironstone quar-ried in the Cottesmore area, home to one of its most successful quarries. When the quarry closed in 1973, a group of railway enthusiasts gathered together in order to preserve and restore what remained of the county's indus-trial legacy. Today, the Museum's collection of quarry stock is probably the most comprehen-sive in the country. The mile line is relaid on the former quarry route where, on "Steam Days", you have the opportunity to ride aboard a restored quarry locomotive.

SEATON TRAMWAY

HOW TO FIND US:
By car: A3052 from
Exeter or Lyme Regis,
A358 from junction 25,
M5 (Taunton)
Car parking: On site in
Pay & Display car park
By rail: Axminster
By bus: Axe Valley Mini
Travel 885 or 889; First
Southern National X53
or No 20
ADDRESS:
Harbour Road, Seaton,
Devon EX12 2NQ
TEL: 01297 20375
WEBSITE: www.tram.co.uk
LENGTH OF LINE: 3 miles
OPENING TIMES:
Easter–end Oct: daily;
Nov–Xmas: w/ends
FACILITIES: Gift shops,
tea rooms, picnic area
DISABLED: One tram is
wheelchair accessible

A RIDE ABOARD a Seaton tram is a wonderful way of exploring the quaint, homely villages and rich green countryside of the Axe Valley. The electric tramway runs for three miles alongside the River Axe (home to a variety of wading birds including oyster catchers, shelduck and grey heron) from Seaton to Colyton via Colyford – the tramway shop at Colyton is an original 1868 railway building. All the trams are purpose-built half-size versions of the trams that ran in Britain's towns and cities before World War II. Tram driving lessons are offered every Friday and Saturday during the season.

SITTINGBOURNE & KEMSLEY

HOW TO FIND US:
By car: A2 between
Gillingham and
Canterbury
Car parking: On site
By rail: Sittingbourne
ADDRESS: Sittingbourne
& Kemsley Light Railway Ltd, PO Box 300,
Sittingbourne, Kent
ME10 2DZ
TEL: 01634 852672
INFOLINE: 01795 424899
WEBSITE: www.
sklr.demon.co.uk
LENGTH OF LINE: 2 miles
OPENING TIMES:
Easter–early Oct: Sun &
public holidays;
Aug: Wed & w/ends
FACILITIES:
Shop, café, picnic area
DISABLED:
No wheelchair access

A RELIC OF Kent's still-flourishing paper industry, the railway was built in 1906 to carry paper between the mills of Sittingbourne and Kemsley to the Docks at Ridham on the banks of the Swale. Two of the original engines are still in use today. Besides being a fascinating historical monument, the Sittingbourne railway also offers delightful scenic rides through the picnic-perfect Kent countryside. The railway holds various special events throughout the year including a "Steam and Beer" festival and a model railway exhibition.

HOW TO FIND US:
By car: Bridgnorth is on the A458; Kidderminster is on the A448

Car parking: Ample at Kidderminster and Bridgnorth, limited at other stations

By rail: Kidderminster

ADDRESS:
The Railway Station, Bewdley, Worcs DY12 1BG

TEL: 01299 403816

INFOLINE: (Talking Pages) free on 0800 600900

WEBSITE: www.svr.co.uk

LENGTH OF LINE:
16 miles

OPENING TIMES:
All year: w/ends; mid-May–late Sep: daily

FACILITIES: Buffet and bar facilities on trains, station bars, tea rooms, giftshops

DISABLED: Specially converted coaches available – please book in advance

THE SEVERN VALLEY RAILWAY not only has more mainline engines that any other preserved railway in the country but, at over 16 miles, also has one of the longest lines. The railway starts at Bridgnorth (hub of the Severn Valley network; pre-booked guided tours of the locomotive works available), a bustling market town and recent winner of the "Britain in Bloom" competition, and stops off at Hampton Loade, from where you can take a walk, via a privately owned ferry, to the National Trust owned Dudmaston Hall with its extensive, landscaped gardens. Another stop is Highley with its perfectly restored, stone built country station, scene of numerous films and television programmes and a good centre for walks, as is the case with the next stop, Arley. The line continues to Bewdley, which has been described as "simply one of the most beautiful towns in England". The final stop is Kidderminster, where there is a Railway Museum.

SOMERSET & DORSET RAILWAY TRUST

HOW TO FIND US:
By car: Just off the A39
Williton to Minehead
road
Car parking: Small car
park by the main road
By rail: Taunton
By bus: No. 28
(Taunton–Minehead)
stops outside the
station
ADDRESS:
Washford Station,
Watchet, Nr Minehead,
Somerset, TA23 OPP
TEL: 01984 640869
OPENING TIMES:
Mar–Oct: 10–5 daily,
when trains are running
on the adjacent West
Somerset Railway
FACILITIES: Gift shop
DISABLED: Call ahead

THIS FASCINATING MUSEUM and photographic archive was set up by railway enthusiasts dedicated to preserving the memory of the great Somerset and Dorset Railway, which ran from 1862 until 1966. There is a vast horde of memorabilia and artifacts on display that helps to paint a vivid picture of one of Britain's best-loved railways. Visitors can watch locomotive wagons and carriages being restored In the engine shed or pull the levers in the reconstructed Midford Signal Box. The Trust organises various events including a model railway exhibition, track bed walks and film shows.

SOUTH TYNEDALE

HOW TO FIND US:
By car: Alston, just off
the A686 Hexham Road
Car parking: On site
By rail: Haltwhistle
By bus: Call Cumbria
Journey Planner, tel:
01228 606000
ADDRESS: The Railway
Station, Alston,
Cumbria CA9 3JB
TEL: 01434 381696
INFOLINE: 01434 382828
LENGTH OF LINE:
2.25 miles
OPENING TIMES: Apr–Oct:
Sun; 23 Jul–Aug: daily;
phone for details of
other dates
FACILITIES: Railway shop
and café (not operated
by the Railway)
DISABLED: A carriage
with wheelchair access
is available, advance
booking recommended

THE JOURNEY ON England's highest narrow gauge railway begins in Alston, just 20 miles south of Hadrian's Wall, and continues through some beautiful North Pennine scenery to Kirkhaugh. The line was constructed on the trackbed of the former BR Haltwhistle–Alston branch and, it is hoped, will soon be extended to Slaggyford. Alston itself, a pleasant cobbled town, was once the centre of an important lead-mining district. You can find out more about the area's rich industrial heritage at the nearby Nenthead Mines Heritage Centre.

HOW TO FIND US:
By car: Buckfastleigh is
on the A38 Devon
Expressway
Car parking: On site
By rail: Totnes

ADDRESS:
Buckfastleigh Station,
Buckfastleigh,
Devon TQ11 0DZ

TEL: 01364 642338

FAX: 01364 642170

WEBSITE: www.
southdevonrailway.org

LENGTH OF LINE: 7 miles

OPENING TIMES:
Apr–end Oct: most days;
Christmas specials

FACILITIES: Café, book
shop, children's play-
ground, picnic sites

DISABLED: Wheelchair
access, adapted toilets;
a restored carriage has
been specially adapted
for wheelchairs

THE SOUTH DEVON RAILWAY is one of the best railways in the country for observing and encountering wildlife. It starts at Totnes and runs for seven miles along the east bank of the River Dart – a fast-flowing salmon river, home to herons, swans and kingfishers. At the terminus at Buckfastleigh, you can watch otters swimming and playing from an under-water viewing gallery at the Otter Sanctuary or walk through clouds of free-flying tropical butterflies at the associated Butterfly Park. Nearby is Buckfast Abbey, one of the most visited religious institutions in the country and the source of an internationally renowned brand of honey. On certain days, a vintage bus links Buckfastleigh station with the Abbey. The railway offers combined railway-otter sanctuary tickets. For a fantastic day out, take a trip with the South Devon Railway and a relaxing cruise along the River Dart between Totnes and Dartmouth (subject to tides).

SPA VALLEY

HOW TO FIND US:
By car: Tunbridge Wells
West is just off the A26
Tunbridge Wells–
Crowborough Road
Car parking: Nearby in
town
By rail: Tunbridge Wells
ADDRESS: West Station,
Tunbridge Wells,
Kent TN2 5QY
TEL: 01892 537715
WEBSITE: www.
spavalleyrailway.co.uk
LENGTH OF LINE: 3 miles
OPENING TIMES: Apr-Oct:
w/ends; mid-Jul–Aug:
Wed–Sun; Christmas
Specials
FACILITIES: Souvenir
shop and café at
Tunbridge West
DISABLED: Wheelchair
access to carriages
available

THE MUCH-LOVED Tunbridge Wells–Edridge line was in operation as a passenger service from the mid-19th century until 1985. In 1996, after much work by a preservation society, it was reopened to the public as a steam railway. At present, the line runs from Tunbridge Wells to Groombridge, home of the Enchanted Forest and Groombridge Place Gardens, with a halt at High Rocks. The ambition is to extend to Edridge. The engine shed at Tunbridge (built in 1891) contains various fascinating examples of rolling stock.

SWINDON & CRICKLADE

HOW TO FIND US:
By car: 2 miles NW of
Swindon, near the A419
off the M4
Car parking: Tadpole
Lane, Blunsdon
By rail: Swindon
ADDRESS: Swindon &
Cricklade Railway,
Blunsdon Station,
Blunsdon, Swindon,
Wiltshire SN2 4DZ
TEL: 01793 771615
LENGTH OF LINE: 1 mile
OPENING TIMES:
All year: w/ends
FACILITIES: Museum, gift
shop and café
DISABLED: Limited
wheelchair access, call
ahead

THE SWINDON AND CRICKLADE Railway Society was formed in 1978 with the intention of rebuilding and restoring part of the then-defunct Midland and South Western Junction Railway. Eventually, they hope to relay four miles of track and rebuild the accompanying signal boxes, engine sheds and stations. Thus far, one mile of track, two steam locomotives and two stations are in operation. Every week-end visitors are invited to come and experience a recreated idyll from steam's golden age: gently puffing trains, whirring signal boxes and quiet rural stations. If you want you can even join in restoring rolling stock or learn how to drive and fire an engine.

SWANAGE RAILWAY

HOW TO FIND US:
By car: On the A351
Car parking: On site
By rail: Wareham
By bus: From
Wareham Station

ADDRESS:
Southern Steam Trust,
Station House, Swanage, Dorset BH19 1HB
TEL: 01929 425800
WEBSITE: www.
swanrail.demon.co.uk
LENGTH OF LINE: 6 miles
OPENING TIMES: All year:
w/ends and school
holidays; Apr–Oct: daily;
Specials in Dec
FACILITIES: (Swanage
Station) Souvenir shop
selling books, videos,
railway memorabilia;
station buffet serving
hot meals and snacks
throughout the day
DISABLED: Wheelchair
access onto trains

SWANAGE, A SLEEPY Dorset coastal resort, is the starting point for the Purbeck-line, one of the West Country's most picturesque steam railways with glorious scenery and historic locations. The line runs all the way to Norden but there is an opportunity to get off and explore the ruins of the famous Corfe Castle en route. A Royalist stronghold during the Civil War, the castle withstood a Cromwellian siege for six weeks, after which it was largely reduced to rubble by Roundhead gunpowder. At the beautifully restored Victorian station of Corfe Castle there is a Railway Museum with many exhibits from the Southern Railway (open on train operating days only). At Swanage station there is a well stocked souvenir shop selling a variety of books, vidoes, and railway memorabilia. The buffet offers hot meals and light snacks throughout the day.

TANFIELD RAILWAY

HOW TO FIND US:
By car: Off the A6076
Car parking: On site
By rail: Newcastle
By bus: X30 from
Newcastle
ADDRESS:
Marley Hill Engine Shed,
Sunniside, Gateshead.
TEL: 0191 3887545
WEBSITE: www.
tanfield-railway.co.uk
LENGTH OF LINE: 3 miles
OPENING TIMES:
Trains run every Sun
throughout the year
FACILITIES: Most trains
have a buffet car,
railway shop
DISABLED: Manual
wheelchair access to
some carriages

BUILT IN 1725 to carry coal from Newcastle's mines to the ships on the Tyne, this is the oldest surviving railway in the world. Steam trains still operate along a three-mile length of track passing through Causey Woods, site of Causey Arch, the world's earliest railway bridge. Tanfield's oldest surviving building is the 1844 Marley Hill Engine Shed, where visitors can watch the ongoing restoration of engines – there is often a blacksmith on hand, forging new parts in the traditional manner. In winter, kids will enjoy the special North Pole days when the trains puff through the beautiful winter landscape on their way to see Santa.

VINTAGE CARRIAGES TRUST MUSEUM

HOW TO FIND US:
By car: On the A629
between Keighley and
Skipton
Car parking: On site
By rail: Ingrow West on
the Keighley & Worth
Valley Railway
ADDRESS: Ingrow
Station Yard, Halifax
Road, Keighley, West
Yorkshire BD22 8NJ
TEL: 01535 680425
FAX: 01535 610796
WEBSITE: www.
neotek.demon.co.uk/vct/
OPENING TIMES:
11–4.30 daily, until dusk
in winter
FACILITIES: Refreshments, museum shop
DISABLED: This museum
gives disabled visitors
(with physical, visual or
hearing difficulties)
acess to all exhibits

A PROP PERSON'S DREAM, the museum's exhibits have been featured in more than 30 films and TV programmes including *The Secret Agent* and *The Railway Children*. It houses a huge collection of beautifully restored late 19th- and early 20th-century locomotives and carriages. This museum tells the story of rail travel for the ordinary passengers: enter the carriages and imagine (or remember) what rail travel used to be like; listen to "Travellers' Tales"; watch the two-hour video presentation. To see trains in action visit the nearby Keighley & Worth Valley Railway (*see* p 39).

WELLS & WALSINGHAM

HOW TO FIND US:
By car: Just off the A149
By bus: Eastern
Counties Buses
ADDRESS:
Wells Next-the-Sea,
Norfolk NR23 1QB.
TEL: 01328 710631
INFOLINE: 01328 710631
LENGTH OF LINE: 4 miles
OPENING TIMES:
Easter–end Oct: daily
FACILITIES: Refreshments, souvenirs
DISABLED: Call ahead

THIS IS THE longest 10.25" narrow gauge steam railway in the world. It runs from the lively North Norfolk harbour town of Wells to Walsingham, the site of a famous Augustinian Priory which, for many centuries, was as popular a centre of pilgrimage as Canterbury. Much of the Abbey was destroyed in the 16th century following Henry VIII's theological breach with Rome, but you can still visit its evocative remains and the pleasant surrounding gardens and woodland. Nearby, the Shirehall Museum houses a restored Georgian courtroom – stand in the dock, sit on the judge's chair or visit the cells before returning to Wells, where refreshments are served in a converted signal box.

WEST LANCASHIRE LIGHT RAILWAY

HOW TO FIND US:
By car: Between
Preston and Southport
Car parking: On site
By rail: Preston and
Southport
By bus: Nos 100 & 102
ADDRESS:
Alty's Brickworks,
Station Road,
Hesketh Bank,
near Preston, Lancs
TEL: 01772 815881
WEBSITE: www.
djrl2ecg.demon.co.uk/
wllr/wllr.html
OPENING TIMES:
Easter–Oct: Sun &
public holidays; Santa
specials in Dec
FACILITIES:
Refreshments, picnic
table, souvenir shop
DISABLED: Call ahead

IN THE 1950s and '60s, Britain's narrow gauge railways, once popular forms of transport for the agricultural, mining and building industries, began to disappear as the country's road network was expanded. The West Lancashire Railway was founded with the intention of gathering and preserving as much as remained of these delightful little railways before they vanished for ever. It has a huge collection of railway equipment gathered from all parts of the country. The highlight is undoubtedly the railway line itself, with the carriages often pulled by the railway's pride and joy, an 1898 Hunslet steam engine called Jonathan.

WEST SOMERSET

HOW TO FIND US:
By car: Bishops Lydeard station is 4 miles from Taunton
Car parking: On site
By rail: Taunton
By bus: 28A
ADDRESS: Minehead, Somerset TA24 5BG
TEL: 01643 704996
INFOLINE: 01643 707650
WEBSITE: www. West-SomersetRail-way.co.uk
OPENING TIMES:
Mar–Jan
LENGTH OF LINE:
20 miles
FACILITIES: Souvenir shops, buffet and buffet car on most trains
DISABLED: Wheelchair access to all stations except Doniford Halt

This charming recreation of a Great Western Railways country branch line is Britain's longest preserved railway. It runs from Bishops Lydeard to Minehead, passing the renowned Quantock Hills and Bristol Channel en route. You may also recognise the immaculately restored station at Crowcombe Heathfield from its numerous film and television appearances. There are museums and displays of engines and stock at Williton, Washford, Blue Anchor and Minehead, whilst Stogumber, Watchet and Dunster are as picturesque as they are historical, with plenty of picnic spots on the beach or surrounding countryside.

WINDMILL FARM

HOW TO FIND US:
By car: On A59 between Liverpool and Preston
Car parking: On site
By rail: Burscough
ADDRESS: The Windmill Farm Railway,
Red Cat Lane,
Burscough L40 1UQ
TEL: 01704 892282
INFOLINE: 07971 221343
OPENING TIMES:
Mar–Nov: 10.30–5 daily; steam on most Sun
LENGTH OF LINE:
0.5 miles
FACILITIES: Museum, picnic area
DISABLED:
Wheelchair access to trains and most of the site

The aim of this recent addition to the list of preservation railways is to establish a working museum of 15″ gauge miniature railways. Opened in 1997, the line now runs from the main farm area to a picnic area and articial lake at Lakeview. A large and increasing collection of rolling stock, coaches and wagons is already on display or undergoing restoration. The resident steam loco is 'Prince William', a 4-6-2 built by Guest in 1949 for Dudley Zoo Railway. Amongst the many items of interest, there is a 1902 vintage Cagney 4-4-0 from the USA, one of only two known to be in Britain.

GROUDLE GLEN

HOW TO FIND US:
By ferry: Services from
Heysham,
call 01524 853802
By car: 2.5 miles from
Douglas
Car parking: at the
beach
By tram: MER trams

ADDRESS:
29 Hawarden Avenue,
Douglas, Isle of Man
IM1 4BP

TEL: 01624 622138

LENGTH OF LINE:
0.75 miles

OPENING TIMES:
May–Sep: Sun;
Jul–Aug: Wed evenings;
Santa specials in Dec

FACILITIES: Gift shop,
light refreshments

DISABLED: Limited
wheelchair access, call
in advance

GROUDLE GLEN was orginally built to indulge the Victorian holidaymaker's penchant for seaside vacations. Today, over a century later, visitors can still appreciate the same spectacular setting and stimulating airs. The original locomotive, "Sea Lion", is once again steaming its way out of the leafy glen towards some dramatic cliff-top views. The journey passes enclosures which once housed sea lions and polar bears as well as a distinctive rebuilt "Swiss chalet" station canopy building at Lhen Coan.

ISLE OF MAN STEAM RAILWAY

HOW TO FIND US:
By ferry: Services from
Heysham & Liverpool,
call 01524 853802
By car: At Douglas
Harbour
Car parking: Douglas
By bus:
calll 01624 663366

ADDRESS:
Isle of Man Transport,
Banks Circus, Douglas,
Isle of Man IM1 5PT

LENGTH OF LINE:
15.5 miles

OPENING TIMES:
Apr–Oct

FACILITIES: Refreshments and souvenir
shops at Port Erin.
There is also a museum
at Port Erin

Disabled: Wheelchair
access throughout
Douglas and Port Erin

THE LONGEST NARROW gauge steam railway in the British Isles takes the traveller on a journey past magnificent coastal views, through charming woodlands and over picturesque hedged meadows to Port Erin. A journey of pure nostalgia – it is like stepping back in time as the line passes through several beautiful, lovingly restored, Victorian stations at Douglas, Santon, Castletown and Port St Mary, finishing at Port Erin, where there is the Railway Museum with an interesting collection of rolling stock and railway memorabilia.

MANX ELECTRIC RAILWAY

HOW TO FIND US:
By ferry: Services from
Heysham & Liverpool,
call 01524 853 802
By car: On the Douglas
promenade
Car parking: On site
By bus:
Call 01624 663366
TEL: 01624 663 366
ADDRESS:
Isle of Man Transport,
Banks Circus, Douglas,
Isle of Man IM1 5PT
LENGTH OF LINE:
17.75 miles
OPENING TIMES:
All year: daily
FACILITIES:
Refreshments at Laxey
DISABLED: Folded
wheelchairs can be
carried, please call in
advance

ANOTHER MANX VICTORIAN survivor, the railway was built in 1893 and still employs two of its original cars – making them the oldest regularly operating electric tram cars in the world on their original line. The line starts on the coast, from where it heads inland to explore glens, hills, and picturesque villages. It stops at many places of interest including the famous wheel at Laxey, the fascinating village of Maughold (alight at Ballajora) with its ancient church and Celtic crosses, and Ramsey, the island's northern "capital". The line provides access to many beautiful walks in the glens and woods of the island.

SNAEFELL MOUNTAIN RAILWAY

HOW TO FIND US:
By ferry: Services from
Heysham & Liverpool,
call 01524 853802
By car: Douglas to
Ramsey Coast Road
Car parking: On site
By rail: Laxey Station is
served by Manx Electric
Railway (see above)
By bus: Isle of Man Trans
port bus goes to Laxey
TEL: 01624 663366
ADDRESS:
Isle of Man Transport,
Banks Circus, Douglas,
Isle of Man IM1 5PT
LENGTH OF LINE:
4.5 miles
OPENING TIMES:
Daily, May–Sep
FACILITIES: Refreshments at Laxey, summit
café, souvenir shop
DISABLED: No special
wheelchair facilities

IT IS 2,034 FT to the top of Snaefell from Laxey there are two ways to get there. You can walk, which would take you the best part of a day, or you can choose the more leisurely option aboard the 3'6" gauge electric Mountain Railway. The six original tram cars, built in 1895, still climb the 1 in 12 gradient and provide wonderful panoramic views over the island's valleys, cliffs and plains. According to Manx tradition the summit affords views of six kingdoms. The first five are England, Ireland, Scotland, Wales and Mann. The sixth is somewhat harder to perceive – it is the Kingdom of God, and is only visible to those whose eyes are clear of hate and full of love.

SCOTLAND

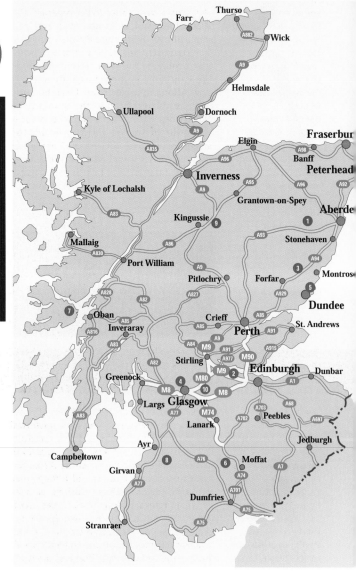

1 Alford Valley Railway
2 Bo'ness & Kinneil Railway
3 Caledonian Railway (Brechin)
4 Glasgow Museum of Transport
5 Kerr's Miniature Railway
6 Leadhills & Wanlockhead Railway
7 Mull Rail
8 Scottish Industrial Railway Centre
9 Strathspey Railway
10 Summerlee Heritage Park

Dᴜʀɪɴɢ ᴛʜᴇ ʟᴀᴛᴇ 19th century the Alford Valley branch line was the focus of a thriving agricultural and granite-quarrying region. The station building, around which the town of Alford grew up, is now the headquarters of the new Alford Valley Railway. From here the line heads north into the grounds of Haughton House, one of the largest estates in the district. Engines include the steam locomotive "Saccharine" named in honour of its years spent working on a sugar plantation (not in Aberdeenshire).

BO'NESS & KINNEIL RAILWAY MUSEUM

Tʜᴇ ʙᴏ'ɴᴇss ᴀɴᴅ ᴋɪɴɴᴇɪʟ Railway Museum aims to give a complete historical overview of the development of the Scottish railway. At Bo'ness is purpose-built exhibition hall in which Scotland's largest collection of locomotives and rolling stock is displayed, as well as various railway buildings relocated from sites all over Scotland. The seven-mile round trip on the railway itself takes passengers to Birkhill, where they may enjoy the ancient woodland of the Avon Gorge, home to a variety of native wildlife including deer and otters, or take a guided tour of the underground caverns of Birkhill Fireclay Mine.

HOW TO FIND US:
By car: Brechin is on
the A933 and just off
the A90
Car parking: On site
By rail: Montrose
By bus: Call Strathtay
Scottish, 01382 228345
ADDRESS: The Station,
2 Park Road, Brechin,
Angus DD7 7AF
TEL: 01674 810318
WEBSITE: www.
caledonianrailway.co.uk
LENGTH OF LINE: 4 miles
OPENING TIMES:
End May–Sep: Sun
FACILITIES: Souvenir
shop and picnic site
DISABLED: Wheelchair
access and assistance

THIS LAST REMAINING section of the former Caledonian Railway branch line
runs from Brechin Station, the line's only
extant terminus and home to a small railway museum, to Bridge of Dun, a good
base for walks along the River Esk to the
Montrose Basin Bird Sanctuary. Also in
the vicinity is the House of Dun, an early
18th-century building owned and run by
the National Trust for Scotland. Currently
one steam and three diesel locomotives
are in service on the line.

GLASGOW MUSEUM OF TRANSPORT

HOW TO FIND US:
By car: 1 mile west of
city centre
Car parking: Facing the
museum
By bus: Strathclyde
Buses nos 6, 6A, 8, 8A,
9, 9A, 16, 42, 42A, 44A,
57, 57A,
By underground:
Kelvingrove
ADDRESS: Kelvin Hall,
1 Bunhouse Road,
Glasgow G3 8DP
TEL: 0141 3311854
WEBSITE: www.
colloquium.co.uk/www/
glasgow/transport.html
OPENING TIMES: Daily
FACILITIES: Café, shop
DISABLED:
Wheelchair access,
adapted toilets,
passenger lift at front
entrance

THE HISTORY OF transport, from horse-
drawn carriages to high-speed trains,
is told in this fantastic museum in Glasgow's twin-towered Kelvin Hall. Its collection of railway locomotives and stock is
among the very finest in Europe. There is
a recreated 1950s' cobbled street scene,
with period shops and an underground
station as well as a cinema that shows
archive film of trams and trains crammed
full of Glaswegians on their way to the
sea. In the Clyde Room there is a model of
every ship built in the famous docks.

HOW TO FIND US:
By car: Arbroath on the
A92 Coastal Route
Car parking: On site
By rail: Arbroath
By bus: Call Strathtay
Scottish, 01382 228345
ADDRESS: West Links
Park, Arbroath, Angus
TEL: 01241 879249
LENGTH OF LINE:
0.5 miles round trip
OPENING TIMES:
Apr–Jun: w/ends;
Jul–Sep: daily;
some Sun in winter;
all dates 1.30–5,
weather permitting
FACILITIES: Sited in West
Links Park, an amuse-
ment area
DISABLED: Wheelchair
access ???

This FAMILY RUN, non-profit-making 10.25" gauge miniature railway is a little gem on the East Coast of Scotland. The track runs alongside British Rail's main line track on the seafront at West Links Park. The highly authentic rolling stock is compli- mented by a miniature bus and fire engine. Starting at West Links Station, the trains pass under a footbridge, on past the signal box, turntable and loco shed, with a level crossing and a tunnel before arriving at Burnside Halt.

LEADHILLS AND WANLOCKHEAD

HOW TO FIND US:
By car: Between
Clydesdale (M74) and
Nithsdale (A76).
Car parking: On site
By rail/bus:Sanquhar.
Bus services run from
the station
ADDRESS:
c/o Alistair Ireland,
23 Pinnaclehill Park,
Kelso, Roxburghshire
TD5 8HA
TEL: 01573 223691
WEBSITE: www.
leadhillsrailway.co.uk
LENGTH OF LINE: 1 mile
OPENING TIMES:
Easter w/end;
May–Sep: w/ends &
public holiday
FACILITIES:
Shop, picnic area
DISABLED:
No wheelchair access

Built on part of a former Caledonian Railways branch line some 1,400 feet above sea level, this is the highest adhesion railway in Britain. It runs from Leadhills, where, in the local cemetery, you can find an obelisk commemorating William Symington and his contribution to steam navigation (as well as the tombstone of William Taylor, aged 137 when he died). The line terminates at Wanlockhead. There are museums at either end containing, respectively, a collection of locomotives from all over the world and an exhibition detailing the history of the region's lead- mining industry.

HOW TO FIND US:
By ferry: Caledonian
Macbrayne: 0990 650000
By car: At Craignure
Ferry Terminal, turn left
on the A849, signposted
By rail: Oban, then take
the ferry
Car parking: Free at
Craignure station
ADDRESS: Craignure,
Isle of Mull, PA65 6AY
TEL: 01680 812494
WEBSITE: www.
holidaymull.org/
rail/Welcome
LENGTH OF LINE:
1.25 miles
OPENING TIMES:
Apr–mid-Oct
FACILITIES: Small shop
at Craignure station
DISABLED: Wheelchair
access; specially
adapted carriage

SCOTLAND'S FIRST ISLAND passenger railway is served by three steam engines, "Lady of the Isles", "Waverley" and "Victoria". There are also 2 diesels and 1 petrol locomotive. From the Old Pier Station at Craignure the trains climb up to the stately home of Torosay Castle where there are beautiful panoramic views of Ben Nevis, the Glencoe Hills, the Island of Lismore and Duart Castle. The island itself is still largely unspoilt, teeming with natural wonders – over 80 species of bird have been spotted, and primroses, wild garlic, rhododendrons, orchids and butterflies flourish in the spring and summer.

SCOTTISH INDUSTRIAL RAILWAY CENTRE

HOW TO FIND US:
By car: On the A713
Car parking: On site
By rail: Ayr
By bus: No. 51 from the
station
ADDRESS:
Dalmellington,
Ayrshire KA6 7JF
TEL: 01292 531144
WEBSITE: www.
btconnect.com/dunaskin
LENGTH OF LINE:
0.5 miles
OPENING TIMES:
Jun–Sep: Sat; Steam
Days some Suns
between May and Sep
FACILITIES: Buffet, book
and souvenir shop
DISABLED: Wheelchair
access to Centre and
trains

BUILT ON THE site of the old Minnevey Colliery, the Centre celebrates the rich tradition of ironworking and coal mining in the area and, in particular, the role played by the railways in the development of these industries. The Dalmellington Iron Company began operations at Dunaskin in 1845, and Minnevey was part of the network of industrial railways that supplied coal for the ironworks – there were steam trains running here as late as 1978. Guided tours round the Centre relate the history of the railways, and visitors can also see a collection of memorabilia in the small museum.

A WONDERFUL TRIP past heather-clad hills, mist-covered lochs and fast running streams on Scotland's premier Highland railway. It runs from the modern skiing resort of Aviemore to the traditional country village of Boat of Garten, just over five miles away. Here, at a viewing site three miles from the station, you have the opportunity to catch a glimpse of one of Scotland's few remaining breeding pairs of ospreys. Perhaps the best way to appreciate the stunning scenery is aboard the restaurant car – formerly a carriage on the "Flying Scotsman" – You can also go monster-hunting at Loch Ness, just 20 miles away.

SUMMERLEE HERITAGE PARK

A 22-ACRE SITE with Scotland's only working electric tramway. It also has an open-top tram from 1910, and more modern cars from Europe. A Glasgow Corporation car is currently under restoration. Static rail stock includes a South African Railways 1956 North British Loco Co built GNAM class 4-8-2+2-8-4 unit. Industrial locomotives, also static, include a Hogg 0-4-0T from 1898 and a Clarke 0-6-0T from 1909. There is a huge exhibition hall with working machinery and displays, and a recreated mine with miners' cottages. A few minutes walk away is the Monklands Canal.

WALES

1   Bala Lake Railway
2   Brecon Mountain Railway
3   Caernarfon Railway
4   Conwy Valley Railway Museum
5   Corris Railway Museum
6   Fairbourne & Barmouth Steam Railway
7   Ffestiniog Railway
8   Great Orme Tramway
9   Gwili Railway
10 Llanberis Lake Railway
11 Llangollen Railway
12 Pontypool & Blaenavon Railway
13 Teifi Valley Railway
14 Snowdon Mountain Railway
15 Talyllyn Railway
16 Vale of Glamorgan Railway
17 Vale of Rheidol Railway
18 Welsh Highland Railway (Porthmadog)
19 Welshpool & Llanfair Light Railway

BALA LAKE

THIS DAPPER LITTLE line, built to link the industrial borderlands with the Cambrian coastal resorts, runs along the shoreline of Wales' largest natural lake. The ride offers unforgettable views of deep river valleys, tranquil water meadows, sheep-dotted hillsides and, of course, the majestic splendour of Bala Lake itself. The headquarters at Llanuwchllyn features an original Great Western signal box, while the main intermediate station, at pretty Llangower, is a popular picnic and walking spot. The more active among you may like to try the range of watersports available at Bala Lake.

BRECON MOUNTAIN

BUILT ON THE trackbed of the former Brecon & Merthyr Railway, this narrow gauge passenger-carrying steam railway winds its way through the beautiful Brecon Beacons National Park in South Wales. You can watch old steam locomotives being repaired in the station workshop, take a picnic overlooking the magnificent Taf Fechan Reservoir or pay a visit to Cyfarthfa Castle, a splendid Regency Gothic mansion set in wonderful manicured gardens.

HOW TO FIND US:
By car: Caernarfon is
on A487, a few miles
south of A55 North
Wales expressway
Car parking: Public car
parks in Caernarfon
By rail: Bangor; bus
service 5 links the
station to Caernarfon
By bus: No. 5 from
Bangor; Nos 1 and 2
from Porthmadog

ADDRESS:
c/o Ffestiniog Railway,
Harbour Station,
Portmadog, Gwynedd
LL49 9NF

TEL: 01690 710568

WEBSITE: www.
festrail.co.uk

LENGTH OF LINE: 7 miles

OPENING TIMES: Early
Apr–early Nov: daily

FACILITIES:
Limited souvenir shop
at Caernarfon. Both
Caernarfon and Waun-
fawr have excellent
places to eat.

DISABLED:
Wheelchair access at
both stations. Please
phone before travelling

THE WELSH HIGHLAND RAILWAY, Caernarfon, saw trains steaming out of the
town for the first time on the reopened
line in October 1997. Backed by the Mil-
lennium Commission, 2000 saw the line
extend along the original track bed for
the first time in 60 years from Dinas to
Waunfawr, one of the gateways to the
Snowdonia National Park. The ambitious
project will eventually recreate the 25-
mile link to the Ffestiniog Railway. Starting beneath the shadow of Caernarfon
Castle, the trains climb away from the
harbour into gentle pastureland with
magnificent views of the Menai Strait and
the distant mountains of Snowdonia.
Beyond Dinas the scenery gradually
changes to woodland before arriving at
Waunfawr, with the foothills of Snowdonia towering all around. Waunfawr is an
ideal location for outdoor activities
including walking and riding over miles
of traffic-free bridleways.

CONWY VALLEY RAILWAY MUSEUM

HOW TO FIND US:
By car: Betws-y-Coed
is on the B5106
Car parking: On site
By rail: Betws-y-Coed
ADDRESS:
The Old Goods Yard,
Betws-y-Coed,
Gwynedd
TEL: 01690 710568
OPENING TIMES:
All year: w/ends;
Easter–Oct: daily
FACILITIES: Buffet car
refreshments, book
shop, model and gift
shop, picnic area
DISABLED:
Wheelchair access,
adapted toilets

This friendly, cheerful museum holds a fascinating collection of railway stock and memorabilia including various model train layouts. There's a mile-long miniature railway and a 15″ tramway available daily for passenger rides. Nearby attractions include Dolwyddelan Castle, the reputed birthplace of Llewelyn the Great, and the picturesque towns of Llanrwst and Penmachno, home to a working water mill.

CORRIS RAILWAY MUSEUM

HOW TO FIND US:
By car: In Corris village,
off the A487, 5 miles
north of Machynlleth
Car parking: On site
By rail: Machynlleth
By bus: Aberllefenni
and Dolgellau services
from Machynlleth
ADDRESS: Station Yard,
Corris, Machynlleth,
Mid-Wales SY20 9SH
TEL: 01654 761303
WEBSITE: www.
corris.co.uk
LENGTH OF LINE: 0.75
miles (scheduled for re-
opening late 2001)
OPENING TIMES: Easter,
Spring public holidays
&; Oct half-term school
holidays; Jun–Sep: daily
FACILITIES: Light refresh-
ments, play area
DISABLED: Wheelchair
access

The museum's displays explain the history of the old Corris Railway, the first narrow gauge line in Mid-Wales, originally built to transport slate from the quarries of the Dulas Valley to quays on the River Dovey. Later it became a hugely popular tourist line which once carried over 80,000 Victorian holiday-makers a year to the Lake of Talyllyn and the mountain massif of Cadair Idris. There are photographs showing the old trains climbing up through the wooded Dulas valley as well as models of the railway's buildings and rolling stock. Nearby attractions include King Arthur's Labyrinth and the Centre for Alternative Technology, with its own cliff railway.

FAIRBOURNE & BARMOUTH

HOW TO FIND US:
By car: On the A493,
7 miles south west of
Dolgellal
Car parking: Gorsaf
Newydd
By rail: Fairbourne
By bus: no. 28
ADDRESS: Beach Road,
Fairbourne, Gwynedd
LL38 2PZ
TEL: 01341 250362
WEBSITE:
www.fairbourne-
railway.co.uk
LENGTH OF LINE:
2.5 miles
OPENING TIMES:
Apr–end Sep, Santa
Specials in Dec
FACILITIES:
Souvenir shop and tea
shop at Fairbourne
DISABLED:
Call in advance

Fairbourne village owes its existence to this line, which was laid in 1895 in order to transport building materials for the village's construction. It now runs from Fairbourne to Penrhyn Point, although there is an intermediate (but thankfully not a request) stop at Gorsafawddachaidraigodanhedogleddollonpenrhynareurdraethceredigion – the longest station name in the world. It's even longer in English – "The Mawddach station with its dragon's teeth on the northerly Penrhyn drive on the golden beach of Cardigan Bay". At Penrhyn Point the train connects with the ferry across the Afon Mawddach estuary to Barmouth.

FFESTINIOG (WHR)

HOW TO FIND US:
By car: Porthmadog is
on the A487
Car parking: Onsite
By rail: Minffordd and
Blaenau Ffestiniog
ADDRESS:
Harbour Station,
Porthmadog, Gwynedd
LL49 9NF
TEL: 01766 512340
WEBSITE: www.
festrail.co.uk
LENGTH OF LINE:
13.5 miles
OPENING TIMES:
Mar–Nov: daily;
limited winter service
FACILITIES: Souvenir
shop, licensed restaurant at Porthmadog
DISABLED: Wheelchair
access at Porthmadog
and Blaenau Ffestiniog;
facilities on trains by
prior arrangement

Past mountain lakes and waterfalls, through wide river valleys and thick oak forests, the unique, historic trains of the Ffestiniog Railway chug their way through the natural glories of Snowdonia National Park. At its highest point, some 640ft above sea level, the views are quite simply breathtaking, stretching for miles on either side. Built in 1832 to carry slate from the mountain mines of Blaenau Ffestiniog to the port of Porthmadog, this is the oldest passenger-carrying narrow gauge railway in the world. Nearby attractions include the Llechwedd Slate Caverns and the architectural delights of Portmeirion.

GREAT ORME TRAMWAY

HOW TO FIND US:
By car: Llandudno is on the A470
Car parking: 100 yds from Lower Terminal or adjacent to Summit Terminal
By rail: Llandudno
ADDRESS:
Victoria Station, Church Walks, Llandudno
TEL: 01492 876749
LENGTH OF LINE:
Nearly 1 mile
OPENING TIMES:
Easter–Oct: daily, please call in advance
FACILITIES: Shops, café, bar at Summit Complex
DISABLED:
Call in advance

THE VICTORIANS CAME to Llandudno, the "Queen of the Western Watering Places", in their thousands to take the waters and travel on its jolly little tramway. The tramline, Britain's only street funicular, climbs through the charming old town to the Country Park, home to many varieties of rare flora and fauna, as well as Great Orme's famous 4,000-year-old copper mines. At the summit, on a clear day, you can see as far as the Blackpool Tower and the Isle of Man.

GWILI

HOW TO FIND US:
By car: 3 miles north of Camarthen off A484, follow brown signs
Car parking: Free at Bronwydd Arms
By rail: Camarthen
By bus: Local services from Camarthen
ADDRESS: Bronwydd Arms Station, Bronwydd, Camarthen SA33 6HT
TEL: 01267 230666
WEBSITE: www.gwili-railway.co.uk
LENGTH OF LINE: 2 miles
OPENING TIMES: Apr–Oct & Dec; selected days; school holidays: daily
FACILITIES: Gift shop, refreshments; picnic site and woodland walk at Llwyfan Cerrig
DISABLED: Wheelchair access to trains

A STANDARD GAUGE steam railway, operated entirely by volunteers, which follows the route of the former Carmarthen to Aberystwth main line through the beautiful Gwili Valley. Station buildings, coaches and a working signalbox date back to the days of steam. Several 0-6-0 and 0-4-0 tank engines are used to haul passenger trains on the uphill gradient from Bronwydd Arms to the end of the newly-opened extension at Danycoed, stopping en route at Llwyfan Cerrig, where there is a free miniature railway. In addition to normal services, special events are held throughout the year.

LLANBERIS LAKE

HOW TO FIND US:
By car: Off the A4086
Caernarfon to Capel
Curig road
Car parking: On site
By rail: Bangor
By bus: From Bangor
station to Caernarfon;
change for Llanberis
ADDRESS: Llanberis,
Caernarfon LL55 4TY
TEL: 01286 870549
WEBSITE: www.
lake-railway.co.uk
LENGTH OF LINE: 2 miles
OPENING TIMES:
May–Oct: Mon–Fri &
Sun; Jul–Aug: daily
FACILITIES:
Refreshments and
picnic area
Disabled: Wheelchair
access to trains, shop
and café at Llanberis –
please phone in advance

SEE THE SNOW-CAPPED splendour of Snowdon aboard this gorgeous lake-side line. Starting at Gilfach Ddu station in the Padarn Country Park at Llanberis, the trains run along the trackbed of a former slate railway through the Alt Wen woods, home to squirrels, woodpeckers and snakes, over the solidified lava of Volcano Cutting, to Penllyn, stopping at Cei Llydan, a great picnic spot with wonderful views of Mount Snowdon on the way back. At Llanberis you can visit the Dinorwic Quarry Workshops, now part of the National Museum of Wales.

LLANGOLLEN

HOW TO FIND US:
By car: Junction of the
A5 and the A539
Car parking: Market
Street in the town.
By rail: Ruabon
By bus:
Call 01978 266166
ADDRESS:
Llangollen Railway,
Abbey Road,
Llangollen,
Denbighshire, LL20 8SN
TEL: 01978 266166
WEBSITE: www.
llangollen-railway.co.uk
LENGTH OF LINE:
7.5 miles
OPENING TIMES:
All year: most w/ends;
May–Oct: daily
FACILITIES: Souvenir
shop and tea shop
DISABLED: Specially
adapted carriage

THE LANGOLLEN RAILWAY, the only preserved standard gauge line in North Wales, wends its way alongside the River Dee, famous for its salmon, from Llangollen, past the famous Horseshoe Falls, through the 689-yd Berwyn Tunnel to Carrog with its beautifully restored 1950s' terminus. There are many attractive hill and riverside walks from the country stations—from Berwyn a 15-minute walk talks you to the Horseshoe Falls, where the Llangollen Canal leaves the River Dee, or walk through the hills from Berwyn to Deeside Halt. It is the railway's intention to extend the route to Corwen in the near future.

PONTYPOOL & BLAENAVON

HOW TO FIND US:
By car: Off the B4248 between Blaenavon and Brynmawr
Car parking: On site
By bus: Pontypool to Anslow, via Big Pit
ADDRESS: Pontypool & Blaenavon Railway, Council Offices, 101 High Street, Blaenavon, Torfaen NP4 9PYT
TEL: 01495 792263

LENGTH OF LINE:
0.75 miles

OPENING TIMES:
Easter; Apr–Sep: Sun & public holidays; May–Aug: 1st Sat in month
FACILITIES: Souvenir shop, refreshments
DISABLED: Limited access – phone ahead

THE NORTHERN TERMINUS, Whistle Halt, of this volunteer-run railway, stands at 1,300ft and is the highest (and probably most windswept) station in England and Wales. The line upwards from Furnace Sidings is the steepest standard gauge preserved passenger-carrying line in Britain and ensures spectacular starts from the locomotives. Once primarily used to ship coal from Big Pit and other local mines, the line runs through wild and dramatic moorland scenery, home to the hen harrier and peregrine falcon, and containing a mix of relics from the days of steel and coal.

TEIFI VALLEY

HOW TO FIND US:
By car: On the A484
Car parking: On site
By rail/bus: No. 461 bus from Carmarthen
ADDRESS:
Henllan Station, Henllan, nr Newcastle Emlyn, Dyfed SA44 5TD
TEL: 01559 371077
WEBSITE: www.teifivr.f9.co.uk

LENGTH OF LINE: 2 miles

OPENING TIMES:
Feb half-term holiday; Easter–Oct: Sun–Thu & public holiday w/ends; Jul & Aug; daily
Santa specials in Dec
FACILITIES: Café, gift and souvenir shop, Railway Charity shop, picnic area
DISABLED:
Wheelchair access

SITUATED NEAR THE famous market town of Newcastle Emlyn and operating on one of the few remaining sections of the Great Western Railway, the Teifi Valley Railway offers a nostalgic reminder of the history of steam and impressive views of the tree-clad Valley as it travels alongside the banks of the Teifi river and through large expanses of unspoilt woodland. At Henllan station, the starting point for various nature trails and country walks, there is a GWR pictoral museum and the "Dragon" miniature railway which takes a leisurely tour around the station gardens and locomotive sheds.

HOW TO FIND US:
By car: Llanberis Station is on the A4086,
Car parking: Pay and display at Llanberis
By rail: Bangor
By bus: From Bangor station to Llanberis, and alternative routes via Caernarfon
ADDRESS: Snowdon Mountain Railway, Llanberis Caernarfon, Gwynedd LL55 4TY
TEL: 01286 870223
FAX: 01286 872518
WEBSITE: www. snowdonrailway.force9. co.uk
LENGTH OF LINE: 5 miles
OPENING TIMES: Mid-Mar–early Nov: daily; because of snow/ice and winter maintenance requirements, the upper section does not usually open much before mid/late May, until when trains will terminate lower down the mountain.
FACILITIES: Cafés at Llanberis and Summit
DISABLED: Wheelchair users are welcome. Please phone ahead

When the weather is fine, this is one of the world's great railway journeys. Commencing from the picturesquely situated village of Llanberis, the railway climbs over 3,000ft in the course of the five-mile journey to the summit of Snowdon, highest mountain in England and Wales. The line is the only rack and pinion line in the UK, operating on the Abt system and encountering gradients as steep as 1 in 5.5 as it winds its way through the wild and rugged landscape of Snowdonia. On a clear day, you can see not only the glorious splendour of Snow-donia National Park but the Isle of Man and, on occasions, even the green-tinged Wicklow Mountains across the Irish Sea. Four of the original Swiss steam locomotives built in 1895/96 are still hard at work, together with one "new" steam locomotive of 1922 vintage. Nowadays, however, they are assisted by four modern diesel locomotives and diesel-electric car set. Should you feel the need to share your elevated experiences, write a quick postcard and pop it in the highest post box in the UK.

HOW TO FIND US:
By car: Tywyn is on the B4405
Car parking: On site
By rail: Tywyn

ADDRESS:
Talyllyn Railway,
Wharf Station, Tywyn,
Gwynedd LL36 9EY
TEL: 01654 710472
FAX: 01654 711755
WEBSITE: www.
talyllyn.co.uk

LENGTH OF LINE:
7.25 miles

OPENING TIMES:
Late Feb–Mar: Sun;
Apr–Oct: daily;
Specials in Dec

FACILITIES:
Refreshments and
souvenirs at Tywyn
Wharf

DISABLED: Wheelchair
access with adapted
coaches on some
trains; please phone in
advance.

DUE TO CLOSE in 1950 after 85 years of service, this narrow gauge line was saved by the Talyllin Railway Preservation Society, the first such organisation in the world. Not only did these enthusiasts ensure the continued survival of one of Wales' best loved railways but they provided inspiration and impetus for literally hundreds of other rail societies over the succeeding decades. The rich industrial heritage that Britain enjoys today is due in no small part to the efforts of the Talyllyn pioneers. The railway itself, still one of the most picturesque lines in the country, climbs through the thick wooded hills of the Snowdonia National Park from Tywyn Wharf to Nant Gwernol. All the passenger trains are hauled by steam engines and there is a small narrow gauge railway museum.

HOW TO FIND US:
By car: Barry is on the
A4226, just off the A48
Car parking: On site
By rail: Services from
Cardiff to Barry Island

ADDRESS:
Barry Island Station,
Barry Island,
Vale of Glamorgan
CF62 5TH

TEL: 01446 748816

WEBSITE:
WWW.
WalesRails/vogrs.com

LENGTH OF LINE: 800 yds

OPENING TIMES:
11–4 w/ends

FACILITIES:
Refreshments,
souvenir shop

DISABLED:
Call in advance

THE VALE OF GLAMORGAN Railway Company was founded in 1994 to commemorate the enormous contribution made by steam railways to the development of South Wales and Barry in particular. From the restored former station and platform, the Company offers steam-hauled rides over some 800 yards of track, which will extend to over a mile during 2001. There is also a museum and display area and a miniature railway. Visitors may also see locomotives under renovation and repair.

VALE OF RHEIDOL

HOW TO FIND US:
By car: Aberystwyth is
on the A44/A487. Devil's
Bridge is on A4120
Car parking: Available
at Aberystwyth and
Devil's Bridge
By rail: Aberystwyth

ADDRESS: Park Avenue,
Aberystwyth,
Cerdigion SY23 1PG

TEL: 01970 625819

FAX: 01970 625819

WEBSITE: www.
rheidolrailway.co.uk

LENGTH OF LINE:
11.75 miles

OPENING TIMES:
Trains run Easter–Oct;
single journey 1 hour
return journey 3 hours

FACILITIES: Refreshments
and souvenir shop

DISABLED:
Limited, call in advance

IN 1989, THE Vale of Rheidol, the last steam railway still operated by British Rail, was sold into private hands, since when it has been thoroughly restored and is now one of Wales' most popular railways. The journey runs for just under 12 miles, from Aberystwyth across the River Rheidol floodplain and up a steep climb to Devil's Bridge, 625ft above sea level. Here you can alight for a walk to the spectacular Devil's Falls and the famous Devil's Bridge itself – in fact three bridges built one on top of the other, the first constructed, depending on whom you believe, either by monks in the 11th century or by the Lord of the Flies himself.

WELSH HIGHLAND RAILWAY

HOW TO FIND US:
By car: On the A487
Tremadog Road
Car Parking: On site
By Rail: Porthmadog
ADDRESS: Welsh
Highland Railway,
Tremadog Road,
Porthmadog LL49 9DY
TEL: 01766 514040
INFOLINE: 01766 513402
WEBSITE: www.
whr.co.uk/WHR/
LENGTH OF LINE:
0.75 miles (2-mile
extension under way)
OPENING TIMES:
Early Apr–Oct: daily
FACILITIES: Café,
souvenir and book shop
DISABLED:
Adapted toilets

Here, a group of enthusiasts have joined together to rebuild and restore part of the Welsh Highland Railway which ran from 1922 until 1937. Today, you can take a short trip from Porthmadog to Gelert's Farm Works, where you can enjoy a free guided tour, and then on to the replica WHR halt at Pen-y-Mount. The carriages are pulled by a variety of locomotives; some travel behind 'Russell', the original company's sole surviving steam locomotive, while others are hauled by a LYd2 Romanian diesel engine – the most powerful of its type in Britain. There is also an opportunity to ride aboard the "Gladstone" carriage, named after the great Victorian Prime Minister who once travelled on it during a holiday in Wales.

WELSHPOOL & LLANFAIR

HOW TO FIND US:
By car: Shrewsbury
Dolgellau road A458
Car parking: On site
By rail: Welshpool
By bus: Midland Red
Buses to Welshpool
ADDRESS:
Llanfair Caereinion,
Powys SY21 0SF
TEL: 01938 810441
WEBSITE:
www.wllr.org.uk
LENGTH OF LINE: 8 miles
OPENING TIMES:
Apr–Sep: w/ends &
public holidays; mid-
Jul–early Sep and Oct
half term holiday: daily
FACILITIES: Tea room,
book and video shop,
both at Llanfair
DISABLED:
Wheelchair access to
both trains and
platforms,

Locomotives from three continents travel along this eight-mile line, puffing their way through the pretty countryside, past farms and rivers and over startlingly steep hills, giving fantastic views of Welshpool's picturesque scenery. You can take the opportunity to negotiate the hills and bends for yourself on one of the Railway's Driving Experience courses, under the patient guidance of an experienced instructor. Canal boat trips are run at Welshpool, and the famous Powis Castle and Gardens are minutes away from the station.